People of the First Cities

People of the First Cities

By RUTH GOODE
Illustrated by RICHARD CUFFARI

MACMILLAN PUBLISHING CO., INC.
New York
COLLIER MACMILLAN PUBLISHERS
London

Macmillan Publishing Co., Inc.
866 Third Avenue, New York, N.Y. 10022
Collier Macmillan Canada, Ltd.

Map by Rafael Palacios

Printed in the United States of America

10   9   8   7   6   5   4   3   2   1

LIBRARY OF CONGRESS CATALOGING IN PUBLICATION DATA

Goode, Ruth.
   People of the first cities.

   Includes index.
   SUMMARY: Surveys the evolution of civilization
beginning with the settlement of the first cities
by the Sumerians through the rise to power of the
Greeks and Romans.
   1. Civilization, Ancient—Juvenile literature.
[1. Civilization, Ancient] I. Cuffari, Richard, date
II. Title.
CB311.G655   930   77–6279
ISBN 0–02–736430–5

For Daniel and Judith,
my city-born son and daughter

Contents

Years Ago	Mesopotamia	Egypt	Bible Lands
5,500	Cities rise in Sumer; writing invented		
		Menes unites two Egypts	
5,000	Ur, Dilmun trade with India		
		Imhotep builds pyramid at Saqqara Great pyramids built at Gizeh	
4,500	Rulers and their retinues buried at Royal Cemetery at Ur Sargon of Akkad conquers Sumer		
		Capital moves to Thebes	
4,000	Gudea reigns in Lagash Sumerian power revives Hammurabi conquers Sumer and founds Babylonian empire Kassites conquer Babylonia	Hyksos conquer Egypt Thutmose I expels Hyksos	Phoenicians trade with Sumer and Egypt Byblos and Sidon rise Terah and then Abraham lead journey from Ur to Canaan and Egypt
3,500		Hatshepsut reigns Thutmose III takes Canaanite slaves Ikhnaton reigns Tutankhamen reigns	Phoenicians invent alphabet
3,000	Tiglath Pileser conquers Babylonia and founds Assyrian empire	Ramses II builds Karnak Moses leads Exodus	Israelites under Joshua conquer Canaan Kingdom of Israel rises King Saul defeats Philistines King David unites Israel and founds Jerusalem King Solomon makes trade alliance with Hiram of Tyre Tyrians found colony at Carthage
2,500	Ashurbanipal reigns in Assyria Capital at Nineveh Assyrian power ends Nebuchadnezzar rules; capital at Babylon Babylon falls Alexander the Great conquers Mesopotamia	Alexander the Great conquers Egypt Ptolemies reign	Alexander the Great destroys Tyre Hannibal leads Carthaginians against Rome Romans destroy Carthage
2,000		Cleopatra reigns Romans conquer Egypt	
1,500			

Indus River Valley	Sea People of Crete	Heroic Age of Greece	Frontier Lands of Europe
			Kitchen Midden and Great Bog people inhabit parts of Europe (8,000 years ago)
	Cities rise in Crete		Farmers from eastern Mediterranean colonize Danube Valley
			Farmers from western Mediterranean colonize western Europe and build Swiss Lake Villages
			Great Stone Builders build passage graves and megalithic shrines
Rise of cities in Indus valley			
			Beaker Folk arrive from south
			Battle-Axe People arrive from east
	King Minos reigns at Knossos	Achaeans settle in Greece	
Harappa destroyed Mohenjo-Daro destroyed		Mycenae, leading Achaean city, trades with Europe for amber	Stonehenge built and rebuilt Val Carmonica rock pictures record amber-bronze trade
	Knossos falls; Cretan power ends	Achaeans besiege and destroy Troy	
		Dorian Greeks displace Achaeans	Celtic culture spreads westward in Europe
		Dorians found Sparta	
		Greek cities rise on Ionian coast	
		Golden Age begins in Athens Athens loses war with Sparta Athens recovers power Alexander the Great conquers Greece	
			Teutonic tribes settle in eastern Europe
			Romans conquer Celts in France and England
			Rome falls, Teutons conquer Europe

People of the
First Cities

Part 1

Five Thousand Years Ago

This is the story of the people who lived in the first cities in the world: the first builders, businessmen, explorers and adventurers, the first kings, soldiers and sailors.

The people of five thousand years ago ventured far and wide. They traveled in caravans across mountains and deserts, and they sailed in small wooden boats across unknown seas. They went to colonize, to prospect for raw materials, and most of all to trade, to buy and sell. To us their world seems strange, with peculiar ways and beliefs. But it was the beginning of our own world of cities, commerce and travel. It was a time of inventions, discoveries and great change.

Human beings have been living on earth for more than a million years, but wide-ranging travel, exploration and trade began less than ten thousand years ago. For most of their time on earth, human beings had lived like all the other creatures around them, finding food and shelter as best they could. But gradually they invented new ways of living.

First they became great hunters, stalking and trapping beasts much stronger and fiercer than themselves. They learned to make tools and weapons, something that even the clever apes had never learned to do. They invented languages. They learned to use fire. The women stitched warm fitted clothing from the hides and furs of animals so that the men could go out to hunt even in the terrible winter cold of the Ice Age.

Human beings were different from other creatures in many ways. Fire gave them warmth for comfort, heat for cooking, and light so they could use the hours after sunset to work on their tools and weapons. Because they had language, they could share their adventures and try to find explanations for everything around them; they could learn from their past experiences and plan ahead for the future.

While the men hunted, the women and the older children looked for food close to home. They gathered fruits, nuts, wild grains and roots, small animals and succulent insects. At times when the hunting was poor, foods like these kept the people from starving. This led to the second great change, the change from hunting to farming.

People got their food by hunting and gathering until about ten thousand years ago. Then, on the eastern shore of the Mediterranean Sea, in a small corner of the world that we now call the Middle East, the change began. The people discovered that they could plant the grains that the women gathered and that they could tame some of the animals that the men hunted. In this way they could produce their own food instead of having to search for it in the wild.

They became farmers. They gave up following the wild herds and living in caves and camps on the hunting grounds, and they gathered together to live in villages. They built houses of mud bricks or of river reeds plastered with clay. They cultivated their fields and cared for their flocks and herds.

During the first million years of mankind's existence there had never been more than a few thousand human beings alive at one time in the whole world. Small bands of hunters and their families wandered over the great land spaces of Europe, Asia and Africa. If they met other bands, they either hid or fought the strangers for the good hunting territories and cave shelters. Life was hard and dangerous. Not many babies lived to grow up, and not many adults lived beyond the age of thirty.

When people took to farming and living in villages, they prospered. The work was hard but life was much less dangerous than before. People lived longer and had more children, and more children survived to become adults. Populations multiplied. Settlements that began with a few families came to hold hundreds. Villages became towns and towns became cities.

Life in the Cities

City life brought more great changes. In the hunting life, all the able-bodied men were hunters, and in the farming life, almost all were farmers. But in the city, for the first time, people earned their living by working at different trades and professions.

There were potters who shaped clay pots, painted and decorated them, and fired them in kilns or ovens. There were weavers who sat at looms weaving cloth, basket-makers, boatmakers, brickmakers, stonecutters, copper-

ATLANTIC
OCEAN

NORWAY

SCANDINAVIAN
PENINSULA

SWEDEN

U.

BALTIC SEA

DENMARK

New Grange

IRELAND

WALES

ENGLAND

Stonehenge

POLAND

GERMANY

E

O

P

Carnac

DANUBE R.

AUSTRIA

SWITZERLAND

CARMONICA VALLEY

ALPS

PO R.

ROMANIA

DANUBE R.

BULGARIA

YUGOSLAVIA

BLA

R

FRANCE

U

PYRENEES

ITALY

Rome

PORTUGAL

SPAIN

E

SARDINIA

Carthage

MOROCCO

MEDITER

RANEAN

SICILY

TUNISIA

Nea
Nikomedia

GREECE

ISTHMUS OF
CORINTH

ITHACA

Athens

Mycenae

Sparta

CRETE

HELLESPONT

Troy

ANAT
PENIN

AEGEAN
SEA

LYDIA

Knossos

Gournia

Phaistos

SEA

Alexa

LIBYA

ALGERIA

A F R I C A

* National boundaries as of 1977

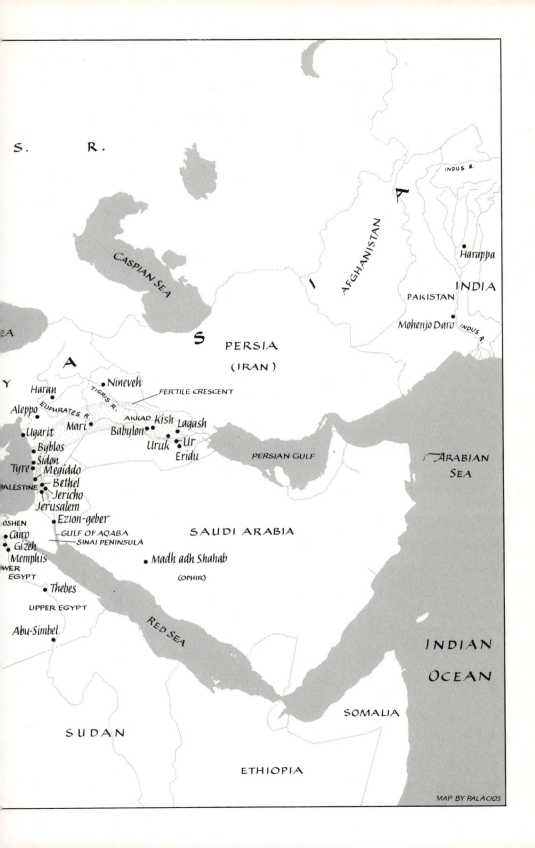

S.   R.

INDUS R.

AFGHANISTAN

Harappa

INDIA

PAKISTAN

CASPIAN SEA

I

S

PERSIA

(IRAN)

Mohenjo Daro

INDUS R.

EA

A

Nineveh

Haran

TIGRIS R.

FERTILE CRESCENT

Aleppo

EUPHRATES R.

AKKAD Kish Lagash

Y

Ugarit

Mari

Babylon

Uruk Ur

Byblos

Eridu

Sidon

PERSIAN GULF

ARABIAN
SEA

Tyre Megiddo

PALESTINE

Bethel

Jericho

Jerusalem

Ezion-geber

OSHEN

Cairo

GULF OF AQABA

SAUDI ARABIA

Gizeh

SINAI PENINSULA

Memphis

Madh adh Shahab

WER
EGYPT

(OPHIR)

Thebes

UPPER EGYPT

Abu-Simbel

RED SEA

INDIAN

OCEAN

SOMALIA

SUDAN

ETHIOPIA

MAP BY PALACIOS

smiths, goldsmiths. Farmers grew enough crops and raised enough animals to feed the people of the city as well as themselves.

The city had rulers who made laws and saw that they were obeyed, so that many people could live together in harmony. The village had also had its ruler, or headman, but city government was a new thing. In the village all the families were related to each other, members of the same great family, tribe or clan. The chieftain of the clan or the patriarch of the tribe, whichever he might be called, was an authority that everyone in the village obeyed. He enforced the law and settled disputes. The older men of the village saw to it that his orders were followed.

But people who lived together in the city came from many different villages, many different tribes. They were not related to each other and they did not owe loyalty or obedience to any single family head. And so a new kind of ruler was needed for the whole city. The early city rulers were priest-kings who ruled in the name of the god that protected the city.

The city also brought about the invention of writing. The men who did the writing, called scribes, were part of a completely new profession. Writing had not been necessary for telling stories or poems, for recounting the history of the people or the deeds of their heroes. These had been told and retold, remembered by the elders and passed on to the children.

Some form of written record was needed to keep track of all the business of city life. People sold what they made and bought what they needed. They owned property. They had land, workshops, tools, houses and furniture. They paid rents and earned wages, not in money—for money was not invented until much later—but in crops and goods and labor.

Records had to be kept of all these transactions. Some of the oldest writing that has been found consists of accounts, written on clay tablets, of bushels of grain, numbers of oxen or sheep or donkeys, quantities of bricks or clay pots, jars of oil or wine, days of labor. The invention of writing came very early in the life of the city.

The Travelers

Most of the people of that time stayed at home in their cities, towns and villages. Few left the place where they were born. But some adventurous men did not like to stay at home, and they traveled great distances and brought back new products and ideas.

These men went on long journeys far from home, over rugged mountains, across dangerous seas. They went because they loved adventure, but there were practical reasons, too. The people in the city needed oil for cooking, timber for building, cloth for clothing, metals for weapons. They wanted all kinds of raw materials for their craftsmen that could not be found nearby. At the same time, the city craftsmen were producing more pots, or cloth, or other kinds of merchandise than the city's own people could use, and so they had something to sell. A village or a town can often live independently, producing everything it needs and using all it produces. But a city lives and thrives on trade with other cities and peoples far away.

Some cities became famous all over the ancient world for fine workmanship in some kind of craft or for some special product. One such product was a richly colored dye for fine cloth, Tyrian purple from the Phoenician city of Tyre, that was bought by kings and rich men all around the Mediterranean.

Kings and queens sometimes sent out expeditions of explorers and traders. More than three thousand years ago Queen Hatshepsut of Egypt sent an expedition from her palace on the Nile, deep into the mountain wilds of central Africa. Its purpose was to trade with the tribal chieftains for elephant tusks used to make the carved ivory boxes, statuettes, jewelry and furniture decorations that the Egyptians liked so much. King Solomon of Jerusalem and King Hiram of Tyre became partners in building a fleet of ships, and sent them across the Red Sea to Africa and India for gold and silver, ivory, apes and peacocks. People began taking such journeys when there were still no roads, no maps or navigating charts. Most of the land was still a pathless wilderness, and most of the seas were unknown.

Sometimes whole families were persuaded to set out for faraway places to establish trading posts in the distant lands where the ships from their home city could exchange manufactured goods for the raw materials the city needed.

Many different peoples lived in the world of five thousand years ago. They spoke different languages, followed their own religions and had their own ways of life. But for the first time men were reaching out toward each other, curious about each other's ways, interested in each other's skills and inventions.

They did not always reach out peacefully. The first cities also brought the beginning of armies and wars of conquest. One city might rise to great power only to be conquered and destroyed by the armies of another. But in spite of rivalries and battles, men were linking their ways of life across land and sea, trading both goods and ideas.

Reading the Books of the Past_____

How do we know all this about the world of five thousand years ago? We know it from the work of archeologists, explorers of the past who go out with spades, shovels and a great deal of special training, and actually dig the story of ancient times out of the earth.

Wherever human beings have lived, they have left traces. Clues—even to the early manlike creatures of more than a million years ago—have been found in caves, canyons and ravines, on riverbanks and lake shores. Usually a hill or a mound is all that can be seen of an ancient human dwelling or a place of burial. Sometimes a modern town or city stands on top of an ancient one.

Often the villagers who live near a buried ruin have tales and legends about the people who lived there long ago. These tales are usually full of imagination and magic. A king whose palace once stood where now there is only a mound may be remembered as a sorcerer or as a hero with a magic sword or a helmet that made him invisible. His people may be recalled as giants, monsters or demons. An ancient graveyard may be considered especially dangerous. The people living nearby believe that angry spirits may rise up if their resting places are disturbed. Nevertheless villagers often dared to dig in the ruins for treasures to sell. Most ruins and old burial places were robbed of their precious objects long ago.

Local legends and folk tales have guided archeologists to many ancient places. Holy scriptures like the Bible and the Vedas of the Hindu religion, and great epic poems like the *Iliad* and the *Odyssey* have also turned out to be quite accurate guides to the sites of buried ruins.

Cities leave the richest ruins: temples, palaces, shops, streets and city walls. But archeologists have also found the outlines of village huts that were made of grass and dried mud. They have found floors of beaten earth, little fireplaces of stones with the ashes of ancient cooking fires still in them, cereal grains and the bones of animals from ancient dinners. They have found some of their most interesting clues to past ways of life in the dump heaps where people threw their broken pottery and kitchen rubbish.

Archeologists dig in these mounds with great care.

They measure and draw sketches as they go, and they sift every bit of earth that they dig out. Sometimes a tiny bead or a fragment of a statue turns out to be a valuable clue in the detective story of the past. Often they find that towns and cities were built successively on the same spot, one on top of the other, over many thousands of years. They dig down through these layers, and they read the story of the past layer by layer.

By five thousand years ago there were already flourishing cities. We know them from their ruins, which have been dug out of the ground after being buried under drifting soil and accumulated rubbish for thousands of years. From the ruins of city walls, houses and storehouses, temples, palaces, counting houses, workshops, even libraries, we can rebuild the ancient cities in our imaginations. We can tell how they looked and how the people lived in them.

A View of the World

Five thousand years ago, most of the world was still a great wilderness of forests, plains, deserts and mountains, most of it uninhabited. But there were small bands of people on every continent, scattered over great distances and usually widely separated from each other.

Some people still lived by hunting and fishing. Tribes of hunters roamed the plains and forests of northern Europe, Asia and North and South America. The people on the American continents were descendants of the ancient cave men from Asia, who had migrated to the New World during the Ice Age thousands of years earlier when a land bridge connected northern Asia to Alaska, where the Bering Straits now are.

There were farming and fishing villages in Mexico and Central America and on the coast of Peru. Farmers were settled in the valleys of Africa, along the rivers of India and China and scattered all over Europe, living in clearings in the thick forests. There were herdsmen tending their flocks in the hills, and wandering tribes driving their herds on the grassy plains. There were families traveling slowly with their children and all their belongings, moving to new dwelling places, walking the forest trails, trudging over the plains and deserts, paddling in dugout canoes along the rivers. Ships with sails and rows of oarsmen traveled long distances on the seas.

One little corner of the world was already crowded. That was the land stretching from the river Nile around the eastern shore of the Mediterranean Sea north to the land now called Turkey, and eastward across the mountains into the valley of the two rivers, the Tigris and the Euphrates. The great cities arose first in this part of the world—it is the place where the modern world of trade and travel, wars and armies, writing and science was born.

At the western edge of this part of the Mediterranean was Egypt, with rich farmland watered by the Nile. At the eastern edge was Mesopotamia, the land between the two rivers, where the Babylonians and Assyrians lived. Eastward, beyond the mountains of Persia, lay the fertile valley of the Indus River, in the land we now know as India. That country was called Meluhha by the inhabitants of the Mediterranean, and city merchants sent caravans over the mountains and ships along the shore of the Indian Ocean to trade with the Indus valley people.

Europe was a wild land, but the people of the eastern Mediterranean knew a good deal about it. On a mountain pass in Switzerland, deep in the Alps, merchants from the cities in the East met with tribesmen of the northern forests to trade for furs and for the precious amber from the shores of the Baltic Sea far to the north. Men in small wooden ships sailed the length of the Mediterranean to the Rock of Gibraltar, then up the coast of Europe to Britain and Ireland. As they went they traded copper and later bronze daggers for the raw copper and tin, and sometimes gold, that the wild tribesmen had dug out of the hills and riverbanks.

Meanwhile people in the settled lands of the East were on the move. For a long time, two great new waves of people had been coming into the cities and towns in the eastern corner of the Mediterranean. One group came from the desert peninsula of Arabia in the south and the other from the steppes and plains of Asia to the north.

These were wandering peoples, shepherds and goat herders and camel riders in the south, cattle herders and horsemen in the north. The southern people belonged to a branch of the human family called the Semites, and the northern people are called the Indo-Europeans. From these two groups of wanderers we have inherited most of our languages, our laws and our great religions.

Part 2

People of the Two Rivers

More than six thousand years ago people were living in cities. These cities, the first true cities we know of, existed in that part of Asia that is nearest to Europe and Africa, the part that forms the eastern shore of the Mediterranean. Eastward from that shore there are mountain ranges and then a broad plain. Two great rivers flow across the plain, rising in the mountains and running southeast into the Persian Gulf. They are the Euphrates and the Tigris rivers, and the name of the land between them, Mesopotamia, is a Greek word meaning "between the rivers." It is in the southern part of this land between the rivers that the first cities were born.

Elsewhere in the Middle East at that time there were farm villages, some of them quite large, and there was even a walled town, named Jericho, which was already two or three thousand years old. But the cities in Mesopotamia were true cities with a central government, a population of several thousand people working at different crafts and professions, and merchants who traded far and wide.

Until about twenty-five thousand years ago the land in the Middle East was green, with forests growing on the hillsides and grasses on the plains. Herds of big grass-eating animals wandered about it, and the people lived by following and hunting the herds. At that time nearly half the world north of the Equator lay frozen under the ice of the last Ice Age. As the ice melted away to the north, the cool rainy winds also moved northward and this part of the world became warmer and drier. The grasslands began to wither, and without those vast pastures the herds of big game dwindled. As the game became scarce, people began to catch and tame some of the animals and keep their own herds of goats, sheep and cattle. And they began to plant and cultivate seeds of the barley, millet and wheat that they used to gather wild.

This part of the world had good land to begin with, and it has been called the Fertile Crescent. There were wild grains and animals that could be domesticated, navigable rivers and nearby coasts along the Mediterranean Sea and the Persian Gulf where men could easily travel by boat, carrying goods for trade. And so the new way of life developed rapidly. After perhaps a million years of following the game and camping in caves on the hunting grounds, and a few thousand years of farming and village life, there were cities.

For a long time, since about twelve thousand years ago, men had been living and farming along the two rivers and on the plains between them. The Euphrates was fairly moderate and gentle in its flood season, but the Tigris was a wild river that often overflowed its banks and flooded the plain, destroying the farmers' houses and crops and carrying away the farm animals.

The history of the oldest cities actually begins with a flood like the story of the Flood in the Bible. In the Bible story the whole world was covered with water, and all living things were swept away, except Noah and his family and the animals that he had taken with him, two by two, into the Ark.

The ancient people of Mesopotamia told the same story, and they also had a hero who was saved from the flood, whom they called Ziusudra. Modern archeologists have discovered traces of a number of floods, and one that was especially severe in which the river waters spread over the plain to such a depth that they must have carried everything away. To the people who lived there, it must have seemed that the whole world was under water.

After the flood the people who survived rebuilt their houses and restored their farmlands. It was then that civilization as we know it began.

The Cities of Sumer

The first city people were the Sumerians and their part of the land between the rivers was called Sumer. No one knows exactly where they came from. They may have wandered from the east, from what is now Iran or perhaps from India. They were probably hunters when they first came to the plains of southern Mesopotamia, and there they turned to farming.

On the arid Mesopotamian plains the people became skillful at making use of the river waters. Working in teams, they dug canals and irrigation ditches to water their fields. As in their hunting days, they lived and worked together as large families, tribes or clans. Each clan had its own protecting god, to whom the clansmen built a shrine. As their farming prospered, periodically they showed their gratitude to their god by building him a larger and grander shrine.

Eventually the shrine became a temple, and some of the members of the clan became priests, devoting all their time to caring for the temple and conducting the ceremonies of worship and sacrifice. The people built houses around the temple, and gradually what began as a farming village grew into a town. The townspeople then began to trade up and down the rivers, selling grain to people such as the hill people who did not have level fields to farm. In exchange they took the timber they needed for building, and later the copper, for tools and weapons, that the hill people mined out of the mountains. In this way the town became a city.

About fifty-five hundred years ago there were five or six such cities in Sumer. Kish, Eridu, Lagash, Ur, Uruk were some of their names. Ur is mentioned in the Bible as the city where Abraham, the first patriarch, was born.

The people of all these cities were Sumerians. They all spoke the same language, built the same kind of temples, houses and city walls, had the same system of city government. But each city was an independent city-state. There was no idea yet of a nation with a central government that ruled over an entire land.

Each city, together with all the farmlands around it, belonged to its own city god and was governed by the god's priests. The priests divided up the farmland, collected the god's share of the crops and herds, gave loans that were paid back in labor or farm produce. They managed workshops where the craftsmen of the city made the tools and utensils for the temple and the city.

The priests were the managers, bankers and supervisors of most of what went on in the city. They were the chief employers of workmen and farmers. When the city needed soldiers to protect it, the priests raised the army and appointed its general. When there was a disagreement between people in the city, the priests were the judges. The most able young men entered the priesthood.

The temple was the center of all activity. Standing high above the busy city, it was surrounded by a compound of offices, workshops, storehouses, courtyards, kitchens, ovens, clay kilns, copper forges and the dwellings of the priests. The temple was of a design peculiar to the Mesopotamian culture, and it was called a ziggurat. It was shaped like a pyramid and built up in a series of steps or terraces to a flat top. On this lofty platform stood the temple proper, an oblong building with an entrance at one end and the sanctuary with its altar at the other. The White Temple at Uruk, dedicated to the sky god Anu, stood on a ziggurat forty feet high.

Broad stairways led up the sides of the ziggurat to the temple doors. We can imagine the people on a holy day, swarming along the main avenue that led through the center of the city and gathering at the foot of the ziggurat steps. There they would watch the procession of priests and high officials as they climbed to the temple to pray and to make the city's offering to its god.

Building stone was scarce in the Mesopotamian plains,

and it was used mainly for the temple foundations. The ziggurat was built of baked brick, plastered over. On the plaster there were elaborate decorations worked in designs of many colors. The designs were made by setting clay nails into the plaster so that only their heads showed. The nail heads were brightly colored, and the pattern of the decoration was formed by these bright, shining spots.

The ziggurat of the great temple at Uruk was entirely covered by designs made of hundreds of thousands of nail heads. The temple entrance had a double row of eight columns which were decorated somewhat differently. The columns were made of palm tree logs coated with a kind of tar. They were covered from top to bottom with designs made by setting shaped pieces of pink limestone, shell and mother-of-pearl into the tar before it hardened. The ziggurat and temple must have been a dazzling sight in the bright Mesopotamian sun.

When a temple was destroyed by fire or flood or a new and finer temple was to be built, it was always built on the same spot, a spot that was considered sacred as the permanent house site of the god. The old temple was pulled down and the statues and amulets belonging to the god were laid in the rubble. Offerings of milk and honey were poured over them, and then the new temple was built on top of the old one. Sometimes four or five temples might lie under the one that was standing, and the same temple site might be used for two thousand years.

Life in the City_____

Mesopotamia is not a gentle land. Rain falls there only in winter, and for the rest of the year, except during the flood season, the land lies dry and baking in the sun. Winters are cold. Fierce winds blow across the plains, and sometimes the winds raise great dust storms.

Life was rugged on the plains, and the people had to be rugged too. The Sumerians were short, stocky, strongly built people. In their decorations on buildings and pottery they pictured themselves as thick-set and fleshy, with broad faces and beak-shaped noses.

For protection against their climate they had to have well-built houses. The plains of Mesopotamia had neither forests nor building stone, and so they learned how to make sun-baked bricks out of the clay soil and later to bake the bricks in ovens in the same way that they baked their clay pots.

They also needed warm clothing to protect them from the winter cold. The Sumerians learned to clip the thick pelts of their sheep and goats, comb it out and spin it into yarn. They wove warm woolen clothing, woolen mats for their floors and woolen blankets for their beds.

A Sumerian city might be laid out with a few streets besides the broad central avenue. On the finer streets the rich had their brick houses. A rich man's house was usually built on a little mound above the street, and only its windowless walls could be seen from the outside. All the rooms in the house faced inward onto a central courtyard. The outer walls might have tile decorations, and the inside walls of the rooms were plastered, painted with decorations, or paneled with imported wood. The furniture was rarely more than a built-up platform for a bed and benches for sitting. There was a table of some kind, and sometimes the master of the house had an armchair with feet carved in the shape of lion's claws.

Most of the houses were not so grand as this. Little houses with only a single room clustered along the winding alleys. These houses were built of river reeds woven together and plastered over with mud, and their roofs were thatched with reeds and mud plaster. These were the homes of the working people and the farmers.

There were also slaves. Anybody could be captured and taken as a slave when his town or city was raided by an enemy or when his side was defeated in a battle. When a town was captured, it was usual to kill all the grown men and take the women and children as slaves.

A poor man might have to work as a slave to pay off his debts, or he might sell some of his children, even his wife, into slavery because he could not support them. Still another custom was to kidnap boys and girls from neighboring tribes to sell as slaves. There was a word in Sumerian writing that combined the sign for a mountain and the sign for a female. The word meant slave girl, because the Sumerians used to kidnap girls from the mountain tribes to serve as their slaves.

In ancient times it was a misfortune to be a slave, but it was not a disgrace, and one was not necessarily a slave for life. A person could work out his time and buy his freedom. The temple priests often loaned a man the price of his freedom, and he then worked out the debt for the temple. It was also customary with some masters to grant a slave his freedom as a reward for loyal service.

Merchants and Traders

Trade was a vital part of the life of the city. A city needs many kinds of raw materials, and the Sumerians traded up and down their two rivers, back and forth across the mountains and across the Persian Gulf to the Arabian coast. A very lively trading center grew up on an island off that coast which was then called Delmun, and is now a tiny independent land, rich in oil, called Bahrein. Merchants from the Sumerian city of Ur sailed to Delmun to trade for luxurious products from Africa and from India. In exchange for their own products, they bought elephant ivory, precious stones, oils and spices.

River boats carried bales and bags of trade goods between the Sumerian cities and the northern mountains, and when the rivers were in flood the merchants led trains of laden pack animals along the shore. Their beast of burden was the onager, a wild ass native to Mesopotamia, almost as large as a horse.

The mountain people needed wheat and barley, and the Sumerian farmers raised enough of these grains on the plain for their own use and for the merchants to trade in the mountains. The city merchants bought luxuries from the mountain people: forest timber and fine limestone for building and precious and semiprecious stones for jewelry.

The most important trade item was the copper that the mountain villagers dug out of the rocky hillsides. The city people needed copper for their tools, and copper was also the most valuable product the Sumerian merchants had for sale in the foreign markets.

In the world of five thousand years ago metals were being discovered in different places, and men were learning how to shape and use them. Gold was washed out of rivers, and silver and copper were dug out of mountains. People also occasionally found iron in a natural state, for instance in a burned-out shooting star called a meteorite, and they would hammer a tool or a weapon out of it.

Iron was extremely rare and very hard to shape into tools. Gold and silver were soft metals, and they were also rare and very beautiful, so they became precious metals out of which jewelry and fine objects were made, like a drinking cup for a king or the hilt of a chieftain's dagger. Gold and silver were also used for sacred statues, and for cups and bowls to use in the temples.

Copper was not so rare, and although it was soft compared to iron and the metals we have today, it made good tools. Stone tools were still being made and were used over most of the world of that time, but good stone was also becoming hard to find, and copper was in great demand. This period in history is called the Chalcolithic Age, from two Greek words, *kalko,* meaning "copper," and *lithos,* meaning "stone," because both copper and stone were in use. Later on men found that copper melted together with another metal, tin, would make a much harder and more satisfactory metal for their tools. This blend, or alloy, of the two metals is bronze, and there was a long period in the story of men's inventions that we call the Bronze Age. Still later came the Iron Age, when people had learned to mine iron ore and smelt the metal out of it, and then forge the iron into shape by heating and hammering it.

At the time when the cities first flourished, copper was the metal men wanted for their tools. Copper was so important to the Sumerian cities that they called their river the Urudu, the Copper River. Euphrates, the Greek name for it, came much later.

Tools of the Mind

The craftsmen needed copper tools but the merchants and businessmen, the priests, the overseers and the managers all needed tools of a different kind. They needed tools of the mind.

The Sumerians invented these tools. To keep count of days of labor, wages of workmen, bushels of wheat, they invented a system of numbers.

Of course people had been counting for thousands of years. They had first counted on their fingers. Even now, when primitive people who have no system of numbers have to count to more than ten, they stop counting and say simply that there are "many."

The Sumerians invented the system of counting by tens and parts of ten which we call the decimal system. The Sumerians used fractions, too, up to one-sixty-fourth.

They had a system of weights and measures: pounds of copper, bushels of grain, quarts of milk or oil, feet and yards of cedar or cypress timber. Their names and units of measurement were of course different from ours.

Another of their measurements, which we still use, is for a curve or an angle, and this is based on dividing a circle. They divided a circle into sixty parts. They invented this form of measurement in their studies of the stars and planets. The Sumerians believed the heavenly bodies had control over human events, and they studied the stars and planets in order to make predictions from them. Their observations and measurements were the beginning of the science of astronomy.

The Sumerian calendar was probably invented in order to keep track of religious festivals so that the proper prayers and sacrifices could be offered to the gods to make sure of good crops and healthy herds. But the calendar was also useful for counting days of labor for which workmen had to be paid. It was useful in measuring distances. A certain town or village would be so many days' journey away.

Businessmen, merchants, managers of workshops needed some way to mark their merchandise and their products. We take for granted the brand names and the labels on things we buy, but in ancient Sumer something that served the same purpose had to be invented. The device the Sumerians came up with was simple but so practical that it came to be used throughout most of the known world of that time and for centuries afterward. It was a stamp or seal, carved with a particular design, that could be pressed into soft clay and would preserve the owner's trademark when it hardened.

The Sumerian seals were usually made of stone or metal in the shape of a cylinder, with the design carved all around it, so that when it was rolled on the clay it left a flat picture. One of the oldest cylinder seals, about five thousand years old, belonged to a city temple; it shows a herd of sacred cattle coming out of their barn or shed. Another shows a priest or king standing under the sign of a particular goddess and holding out sacred rosettes to two sheep. Still another shows a bearded hero with a tall headdress, holding two bulls by their throats, one with each hand; nearby a man with the head of a bull is holding two lions. Others show gods and goddesses, often with worshipers offering gifts.

Every part of such a seal had meaning. The animals shown were sacred to a certain god, or the god's sign or standard was shown. A crescent moon on a seal was not merely a decoration, but the sign of the moon god Sin. Identifying the symbols on such a seal was as easy for the people of that time as it is for us to identify the eagle and the picture of George Washington on a United States dollar bill.

Businessmen also needed documents, contracts and agreements. They had to be able to keep records, send out bills, note down loans, payments, wages. For these purposes, they needed a writing system.

The Invention of Writing

Like all great human advances, writing had a small and simple beginning. It began with the potters decorating their clay pots and vases.

Sometimes a potter would merely make a design, like dots, squares, triangles, in a pleasing arrangement. If he wanted to tell a story in pictures, he might only have space on his pot or jar for a kind of picture shorthand. Ancient potters often used stick figures for people and animals, a few lines for a house or tree. They would draw two parallel wavy lines for water, a triangle for a mountain, a star for the sky, a pair of horns for an ox.

That was picture writing, in which the shorthand picture stood only for the particular object that was pictured. The next step came when the figure of two parallel wavy lines was understood to mean not only water itself but the sound of the word. Then two or three such signs could be put together to make a single long word that had the same sounds as the pictures but a different meaning.

The oldest writing that has been found is a limestone tablet of about fifty-five hundred years ago, from the Sumerian city of Kish, and on it are signs for a head, a hand, a foot, and a farm implement for threshing the grain. The signs are still in picture form and we can read the pictures, although we are not able to understand what they say.

A certain kind of puzzle, called a rebus, is made up of pictures that represent words, syllable by syllable. To solve the puzzle you must sound out the object in each picture. For example, you might see a picture of a cape and a picture of a bull, and you would read cape-a-bull, "capable." The word *capable* has nothing to do with either a cape or a bull. The pictures have simply given you the sounds, not the meaning.

The Sumerian language lent itself well to picture writing. It was a language something like Chinese, made up of short words that did not change according to grammar. The word *draw* would not change to *draws, drew, drawing* or *drawn*. It would always be the same. The same picture-sound could also mean different words that sounded the same but had different meanings. The reader would understand which word was meant according to where it was in the sentence and what the sentence was about. For example, the picture sign for an eye could mean "eye" or "I," but the reader would know at once what the meaning of the sign was.

Here are some examples from ancient Sumerian. The Sumerian word for water had the sound A, and the word for the preposition *in* was also A, and so they used the same sign, the two parallel wavy lines, for both words.

They also made the same sign stand for different words with meanings that had some relation to each other. The eight-pointed star meant the sky or heaven, the Sumerian word AN. But the star also meant "high." It could also mean a god, which in Sumerian was an altogether different word, DINGIR. The sign for DU, meaning "leg," looked like a leg, and it was also the sign for several verbs that had to do with using the legs, although they were all different words. The same sign that stood for *leg* could also mean GUB, "to stand," or GIN, "to go," or TUM, "to carry off."

Gradually the picture signs became less like pictures and more like signs. A clerk checking off a cargo boat or caravan while it was being unloaded could not take time to make very elaborate pictures. He had to use signs that could represent in a few strokes the words for copper, gemstones, different kinds of wood and a dozen other products, and a few more strokes for the quantity of each. These signs were more like our writing. But each sign still stood for a whole syllable, a group of sounds.

An alphabet of separate letters that could be combined in thousands of ways to make thousands of words in all sorts of languages was not invented until much later.

As business and commerce developed, the clerks and scribes began to write on tablets made of soft clay instead of carving on stone. They used a pointed writing tool, called a stylus. The strokes made by the stylus on the soft clay were wedge-shaped, and so their kind of writing is called cuneiform, from the Latin words for "wedge" and "shape."

At first the Sumerians wrote in columns from top to bottom and from right to left, the way Chinese and Japanese are still written. Then they began to write in horizontal lines from right to left, probably because that made it easier not to smudge what they had already written. Hebrew and Arabic are still written in this way, from right to left. Some of the early Greek writing went from right to left and then back again from left to right. The Babylonians, who came after the Sumerians in the same part of Mesopotamia, took over their cuneiform writing along with many of their other arts, and were the first to write from left to right, as we and most Western peoples do today.

Thousands of clay tablets from the Sumerian cities have been found. They have lasted through thousands of years as no writing on paper could have lasted. Even in Egypt's dry climate, where everything seemed to last forever, the oldest papyrus rolls that have been found are two thousand years younger than the oldest clay tablets.

Many of the clay tablets from Mesopotamia are business documents, contracts, bills, lists of farm products, records of farmlands. The majority of these belonged to the temple, which handled most of the city's business. But there were also private businessmen in the Sumerian cities, and many of the tablets record their business dealings. There are also tablets like books of literature in a library, with poetry, stories and legends from the past, accounts of historical events in the city, prayers and instructions for performing religious ceremonies.

Some of the clay tablets have lines drawn on them to keep the writing straight, as in a school notebook. And there are tablets with lists of words like dictionaries. One has the names and signs for different kinds of fish, and another for different kinds of dogs. The Sumerians had schools and teachers, and these were the textbooks they used to train clerks and scribes in the special profession of writing.

Living in Sumer

The Sumerians had scholars who taught the city's history, literary men who wrote its stories and poems, men of science who studied the heavens, physicians who treated the sick. We learn about them from the writings on the clay tablets. The most learned men, and perhaps the only ones who could read and write, were the priests. They not only conducted the city's religion and most of the city's business, but were the scientists and the physicians as well.

The Mesopotamians believed that sickness was caused by evil spirits sent by the gods to punish people for wrongdoing, and therefore part of any treatment involved prayers and repentance. A priestly physician was needed to cure the patient's soul. But there were also doctors who came with herbs and medicines to help cure his body.

The tablets tell us much about how the people of Sumer lived fifty-five hundred years ago. They worked for the temple as carpenters, metalsmiths, potters, weavers, cooks and bakers. The herdsmen tended several kinds of sheep, some for wool and some for meat. They also kept goats, pigs, cows and the onagers and oxen which were the beasts of burden. They had meats and plentiful fish, as well as milk and cheese, wheat and barley, dates and grapes. One tablet like a grocer's list records the delivery of quantities of bread and beer to a number of customers.

They had pottery dishes, bowls, vases, pitchers and drinking cups of many shapes and sizes, some with handles, some with spouts. They had plows, nails, axes. They still used the throwing spear and the bow and arrow when they went hunting for lions, wild sheep and deer. They had stringed musical instruments like harps and lyres, and they played the cymbals and the systra, a kind of rattle. They had two-wheeled and four-wheeled carts with wheels made of solid disks of wood, without spokes. No one knows quite where or when the wheel was invented, but it probably developed from putting logs under a heavy burden to roll it more easily along the ground.

The Sumerian clothes are interesting. In most of the pictures the people, especially the workmen, are shown bare to the waist and wearing a short kilt or a somewhat longer skirt. In some temple scenes the priests, bringing offerings, are shown with no clothes on at all, while the king appears in a long skirt with a train trimmed with tassels. Goddesses and women are also shown with the upper part of their bodies bare or with one shoulder draped.

A picture of a royal banquet shows the guests, bare to the waist, wearing stiff skirts that are finished at the bottom with tassels or fringe. Some of the men are bearded, some are clean-shaven. Some have shaven heads and some wear their hair long enough to cover the ears. In one picture a woman, perhaps a dancing girl or a slave, is shown with her long hair tied and hanging down her back. In another, a man hunting with bow and arrow is bearded and wears a turban and a long coat with a wide belt. Men of that part of the world were still wearing this five-thousand-year-old costume early in our own twentieth century, and in remote villages some still do.

As the Sumerian cities prospered, they sent out armies to raid each other's trade routes and sometimes to capture and destroy a rival city. The priest-king of the early days became a warrior-king who led the army in defense of the city or rode out in his chariot at the head of his troops to conquer a rival city. The captains rode in four-wheeled chariots drawn by onagers, and they fought with battle axes and bow-and-arrow. The foot soldiers wore felt cloaks and leather helmets, and they fought with short spears.

One warrior, Prince Mes-Kalamshar, was buried with his helmet on. The helmet, made of electrum, an alloy of gold and silver, was carved like a wig with the hair curled at the sides and fastened in a bun at the back. The helmet was worn over a quilted cap, which extended below the metal edges and was fastened with laces, drawn through pierced holes all around, to keep the metal from chafing the skin. From the Prince's skull, modern scientists were able to tell that this royal warrior of forty-five hundred years ago was left-handed!

The Royal Graves of Ur

The city of Ur, the farthest south on the Euphrates, was for a while the richest and most powerful of the Sumerian cities. The rulers of Ur were buried with all their finest furniture and jewelry, their golden armor and beautifully decorated weapons. The kings and queens of Ur also took their whole human retinue with them into the grave.

In the royal cemetery at Ur there is a tomb of a king who lived about forty-five hundred years ago. In the tomb were the bodies of seventy-four people, the entire royal household. When the tomb was discovered, the court ladies were found lying in a row, decked in their finest robes, with necklaces and jeweled headdresses, just as they had laid themselves down to die, after drinking a potion of some kind, when the tomb was closed over them. The court musicians lay with their hands extended to the strings of their harps. The charioteers lay in their crumbled chariots, still holding the reins, and the grooms lay beside the animals whose bridles they had held.

Among the treasures in the royal cemetery of Ur was a large double plaque of inlaid shell and mother-of-pearl. It is called the royal standard of Ur, and shows Sumerian life, with war scenes on one side and peacetime activities on the other. On the war side, the chariots and the captains, the king with his soldiers and the captives taken in battle are shown. On the peace side are the farmers and their farm animals, men carrying produce on their backs, the king and his family feasting in the banquet hall.

Despite their quarrels with each other and with rival peoples around them, the Sumerian cities thrived for more than a thousand years. Then a conqueror of a different people, Sargon of Akkad, came down to Sumer from the northwestern part of Mesopotamia with his armies and made himself ruler of all that part of the world, east to the mountains of Iran and south to the Persian Gulf. This was the first empire in history, embracing cities and different peoples under one rule.

Sargon and his nation were Semites, a people who may originally have come from Arabia along the eastern Mediterranean shore into western Asia. (The name Semite is a Biblical word derived from an old belief that these peoples were descended from Noah's son Shem after the Flood.) The Semites became a large family of peoples, speaking similar languages and following many of the same customs, but they were also rivals and were often at war with one another. The Babylonians and Assyrians who later came to Mesopotamia, the Phoenicians and the Hebrews of ancient Palestine, were all Semites, as are the Arabs today.

Sargon was the first of a series of Semitic conquerors of Mesopotamia. He ruled for fifty-five years, and his descendants ruled after him for a time. Then they declined, Sumerian leaders rose again, and the cities enjoyed their richest period. Old temples were restored and new temples were built, trade flourished along the two rivers and across the nearby seas, and the people lived in peace under wise rulers.

A Sumerian leader named Gudea began this period of prosperity and peace when he took power in his own city of Lagash. There is an impressive statue of Gudea carved from polished black stone, in which he stands calm and thoughtful, with his hands clasped across his breast, his cloak draped over his left shoulder and arm. He is not a handsome man but his whole appearance is strong and dignified.

Gudea's son ruled after him, and then the power of Sumer passed to the kings of Ur. After about two hundred years of splendor, mountain tribes invaded and conquered Ur, held it for a while and lost it to the next conqueror. This was Hammurabi, who became king of a new city called Babylon.

So ended the Sumerians and their history which lasted nearly two thousand years. The great Sumerian inventions of writing and numbers, their laws and sciences, even their stories of the Creation and the Flood, were all carried on by their successors, the Babylonians. Hammurabi himself passed on to the world the Sumerian legal system in a code of laws.

The Sumerians mingled and intermarried with their conquerors and so became a part of the future. But as a separate people in history they were lost and forgotten, until their cities with the tall ziggurats and temples, their clay tablets with the first writing, and the splendid treasures in their royal tombs were rediscovered by modern archeologists, digging in the ancient plains between the rivers.

New People

Babylonia did not keep its power for very long. Soon after Hammurabi's death it was overrun by a mountain people called the Kassites, who remained in control for nearly six hundred years. During that time a new Semitic people, the Assyrians, came to power in the north, and they were the next conquerors of Babylonia and of all Mesopotamia.

The Assyrians borrowed their arts and sciences, laws and religion from the Babylonians, just as the Babylonians had taken theirs from the Sumerians. But the Assyrians made their great achievement the art of war. The records left by their kings are records of conquests and bloody massacres. They held all the smaller nations between Mesopotamia and Egypt as tributary states. Their cruelty was notorious, especially against any city that dared to rebel.

Although Babylonia was a subject nation under Assyria, the Babylonians continued to develop the arts of civilization. Several times in these centuries an Assyrian king with his war chariots and siege machines attacked Babylon, slaughtering its people and leveling its buildings. But Babylon was always rebuilt.

One Assyrian king, named Esarhaddon, showed generosity to captured peoples. He allowed their cities to stand and their populations to live and work, paying him his tribute and sending him their young men to serve in his armies. But Esarhaddon's son Ashurbanipal again took up the harsh policy of spreading death and destruction. He gained control of the largest empire in Assyria's history, and even took tribute from Egypt for a time.

Ashurbanipal built a magnificent palace at Nineveh, the Assyrian capital on the Tigris River. There he collected a great library of thirty thousand clay tablets which contained the literature and learning of Babylon and ancient Sumer, as well as the history of the Assyrian kings and all their wars.

But the conquest of other peoples finally proved to be Assyria's ruin. Wars ate up the kingdom's wealth. Lands that had been laid waste could not produce crops or animals. Soldiers drafted from conquered nations did not make the most loyal armies. About fifteen years after Ashurbanipal's reign ended, his proud city of Nineveh fell to a Babylonian leader and his allies from the east, the Medes and Persians. The son of this leader was Nebuchadnezzar, the last great king of Babylon.

The Wonders of Babylon ───────────

In Nebuchadnezzar's reign the land of Babylonia covered the same southern region that had been the land of Sumer more than a thousand years before. But his power also extended over nearly the whole of Mesopotamia, from the northern mountains to the Persian Gulf. He controlled the little nations and the trade routes all the way to the Mediterranean shore.

Babylon in Nebuchadnezzar's time was a dazzling city. Its temple ziggurat towered more than six hundred feet high, and the wall around the city was fifty-six miles long and so wide that a four-horse chariot could be driven along its top. The Euphrates River, fringed with palms, ran through the city; a fine bridge spanned it. An approaching traveler could see far across the plains the Hanging Gardens of Babylon, rising like a green and flowery hillside in a part of the world where there were almost no natural hills at all.

The Hanging Gardens were one of the Seven Wonders of the ancient world. Nebuchadnezzar had built them to please a favorite wife in his harem, a Persian princess who was lonesome for the green hills of her native land. The gardens were built up in terraces to a height of seventy-five feet, and soil was carried up to plant not only flowers and shrubs, but full-grown trees. Water from the Euphrates was pumped to the topmost terrace by shifts of slaves toiling around the clock. It watered a lush garden where the royal wives and their waiting women could stroll and lounge in the cool fragrant shade, high above the hot and dusty city on the plain.

The city glittered in the sun, for its bricks were faced with bright glazed tiles of blue, yellow and white, decorated with animals, birds, plants and geometric designs. Thousands of the bricks have been found where the city once stood, and the boastful inscription, "I am Nebuchadnezzar, King of Babylon," can still be read on most of them.

After reigning for about forty years, Nebuchadnezzar was stricken with a peculiar insanity. He believed that he was a beast of the fields, walked on all fours and ate grass. His successor, Nabonidus, was not interested in ruling but in the country's past, and spent his time directing teams of slaves in digging up the ruins of Sumer that lay under the soil of Babylon. Nebuchadnezzar's vast empire lasted less than thirty years after his death, and then the rising new power of Persia took over most of Mesopotamia and held it for many centuries.

In their own thousand years of history the Babylonians developed still further the arts and sciences they had inherited from Sumer. Babylonian mathematicians and astronomers named the constellations and the zodiac and made the first calculations of the motions of the stars and planets through the heavens. Babylonians created a great literature of poetry, stories, laws, inventions and philosophy. Through the Persians, and after them the Greeks, they passed these accomplishments on to the Western world.

People of the Nile

Part 3

Overleaf:
Along the Nile's reedy banks, Egyptians speared the abundant fish and netted game birds in skiffs like these. At the left is a portrait of Nefertiti, Pharaoh Ikhnaton's queen.

The ancient Egyptians called their river Father Nile. They knew that their lives depended on the big, slow river, the only one of Africa's three great rivers that flows northward across the desert to the Mediterranean. The other two, the Congo and the Niger, turn aside at the desert's edge and flow away west to the Atlantic. But the Nile flows steadily on, across miles of burning sand where almost no rain falls year after year.

Until about twenty-five thousand years ago, all this desert was green prairie. When the last Ice Age ended and the moisture-laden winds moved northward, the prairie withered and the rivers and streams dwindled and died.

The Nile did not die. Drenching rains still fell, as they do today, in the Mountains of the Moon high in the heart of Africa. Waters to feed the Nile poured down through mountain gorges and over cataracts, seeped through big swamps and collected again in the riverbed, to flow onward across a thousand miles to the Mediterranean Sea.

As the land withered to east and west, the animals and the people followed the shrinking grasslands until they came to the river. But the herds of big grass-eating animals that once roamed the plains could not survive without vast pastures, and they gradually disappeared. In time the people who had followed and hunted them gave up the wandering life and settled down along the riverbanks. And because the Nile flowed north into the Mediterranean, they eventually became part of the teeming Mediterranean and nearby Asian world of cities and trade.

Even though the big game was nearly gone, the earliest settlers in the Nile valley of Egypt did not go hungry. The river shore was green with tall grasses and reeds and rich in birds, wild fowl and small animals. Fish were plentiful, and so were wild plant foods and wild cereal grains.

The change in climate that so altered the land came slowly, over thousands of years. When they first came to live along the Nile, the people still traveled back and forth between the river and the desert, following the water courses that filled up each year when the Nile flooded. Elephants, wild asses and wild oxen, antelopes, ibex and Barbary sheep still found some pasture there. Lions hunted these grass-eating animals and men hunted both the lions and the grass-eaters.

When the big game became too scarce to be depended on as a food supply, the people turned to smaller animals, water fowl, birds. They tamed the dog, a perfect hunting companion. With its keen sense of smell, a dog could track among the reeds for small game which a man often could not see.

The people began to plant the cereal grains, millet and barley, instead of merely gathering them wild. They tamed the wild pig for food and the wild ox for food and work. Eventually they began to tame the river itself.

Of all the world's great rivers, the Nile is the most accommodating to men's needs. Its flow is steady and its floods are gentle. It wells up over its banks and across the flat bed of its valley, and seeps into the earth. Most other rivers tear away the land when they flood, but the Nile brings tons of new rich earth from the upland plains and swamps, and spreads this good soil over the land as far as its waters reach. And, for men's purposes, the Nile floods at a good time of the year. It begins its slow rise in the summer months. By the fall, when the waters go down and the ground is ready for planting, the time is just right in that climate for sowing the winter crop.

For cultivating this soil, so rich and well watered, the first farmers did not need tools or fertilizers. It was enough just to scatter the seed and tread it into the ground with their feet. Taming the river was also easy. They only needed to dig channels and guide the flood waters to the fields they wanted to irrigate. Later they also learned to store water over the dry season, in artificial lakes that filled up at flood time.

And the climate was also excellent. The warm sun brought good crops out of the rich moist soil, and in the dry desert air the harvested grain could be stored without spoiling.

All along the edge of the valley, beyond the reach of the flood waters, the Nile farmers built their storage granaries. The only danger to their grain was rats, and the answer to rats was cats. Very early in Egyptian history the small wild cats that prowled around the granaries, hunting the rats, were welcomed by the people. As time went by, the cats that guarded the grain became sacred animals in Egypt. It was against the law to harm a cat or to take one out of the country, and when a cat died it was buried and mourned like a member of the family.

The Nile valley had yet another advantage for the river dwellers. Along its whole length it was protected by natural fortifications on both sides. A wall of cliffs, made of hard granite, separated the valley from the desert. Beyond the cliffs stretched the desert, a wasteland that was almost impossible for an enemy to cross.

Only once in its long history was ancient Egypt invaded and ruled by foreigners. The invaders were a wandering people known as the Shepherd Kings, and no one really knows how they accomplished their conquest. Another time, attempting to conquer Egypt, an army simply vanished into the desert. No trace of those thousands of men, their animals or their weapons, has ever been found. The Nile dwellers lived as safely within their green valley as in a fortress.

When the villages prospered and the people had time to become interested in their neighbors up and down the valley, the river gave them a perfect road for travel. Its gentle current carried their boats downstream, and a steady breeze from the north helped them sail upstream.

The Two Egypts

Ancient Egypt had the peculiar shape of a long thin funnel with a very wide opening. Most of the country was the long narrow valley, about five hundred miles long but no more than ten or twelve miles wide on either side of the river, that began at the last of the river's cataracts on its way down from the mountain highlands where

Aswan is now. (This is called the First Cataract, because it was the first that modern explorers came to when they traveled up the river toward its source.) This long valley was Upper Egypt.

Approximately fifty miles from the sea, about where Cairo now stands, the Nile begins to divide. It branches into hundreds of streams, and threads its way across a wide, fertile area. This is the bed of rich silt that the river has carried down across half of Africa and dropped at the place where the Nile enters the sea, and is called the delta. *Delta* is the word for the Greek letter *D*, which is shaped like a triangle, Δ. The delta of the Nile spread out like a triangle along the Mediterranean coast, and formed the wide opening of the funnel. This was Lower Egypt.

The people in both Egypts had the same origins. When they began living along the river, about ten thousand years ago, they were already a mixture of all the different tribes of hunters that had wandered over Africa, Asia and Europe for hundreds of thousands of years.

After their ancestors had settled into permanent villages, the Egyptians gradually evolved into a characteristic physical type. The many pictures and statues in which they portrayed themselves show them as small, slim people with straight square shoulders and narrow hips. The men and women of ancient Egypt, whatever their age, are shown with this trim, slender figure. No doubt there were fat Egyptians, but the slim, small-boned figure was their ideal.

The people of Upper Egypt rarely met strangers from

other parts of the world. They knew only people like themselves, from their own village or other similar river villages. These were the people they met and married, and so they and their children came to look more and more alike through the centuries.

The people of the river villages were also more united than those in the delta. In Upper Egypt it was a simple matter to send tax gatherers and government officials up and down the river, and to unite the villages under one government. The tribal priest or wise man, the one who kept the record of the seasons and could predict the rising of the Nile, became the priest-king of all the valley land of Upper Egypt. The riverbank people could go up and down the river from village to village. They could call men from several villages together when many hands were needed to dig irrigation ditches or build a dam to make a large flood pond for water storage.

In contrast, the delta villages of Lower Egypt were scattered along the many streams and waterways, and they could not easily visit back and forth across the marshy and often flooded land. The people who lived along the coast, however, were more in touch with the rest of the world and learned about new inventions and new ideas. Traders and travelers from other lands came through their villages, and some of these villages grew into sizable seaports. But although they did become organized into districts called nomes, somewhat like our counties, the people of Lower Egypt did not have a strong central government.

A little more than five thousand years ago a priest-king

from Upper Egypt named Menes came into the delta and organized the two Egypts into one country. The Egyptians considered his reign the beginning of their country's history. Menes built his capital, Memphis, at the beginning of the delta where the two Egypts join.

More than a thousand years later, when the Israelites came out of the desert to live in Egypt, they spoke of the ruler not by his name but by his house, in the same way that we often speak of the White House when we mean the President and his staff. They called the king's palace *per-'o,* which means "the great house." From this word we derived the Biblical term *Pharaoh,* the title of the kings of Egypt.

The Country of Forever _____

The Egyptians seem to have realized that they were a most fortunate people. According to their pictures and religious customs, they seem to have believed that life in their sheltered valley would never change and that it need never change. Even when a man died, his soul could go on living in the same way that the man had lived before. The soul would be weighed and judged by the gods of the underworld, and if he had lived righteously and everything had been properly prepared for the life of his soul, he would live on forever.

The preparations for this life of the soul were important. First it was necessary to preserve the body. The Egyptians embalmed the body by means of chemicals and perfumes and wrapped it in many layers of finely woven cotton. Then they laid it in a nest of cases, one fitted within the other. These cases were often beautifully carved and painted with a portrait of the person whose body lay inside. Many of our museums have these mummy cases on display, and some have an actual mummy, the wrapped and preserved body of an Egyptian man or woman who lived thousands of years ago.

The mummy in its case was then laid in a tomb furnished like an actual room or house for the soul to live in. Sometimes there would even be a real garden around the tomb where the soul could walk and enjoy the flowers.

The homes for the souls of Pharaohs and high officials were furnished for an eternal life just like the life that person had lived on earth. There were fine carved and gilded beds to sleep in, chairs to sit on, jewelry to wear, cosmetics for a lady to beautify herself. The little stone bottles of perfume were still fragrant when the archeologists opened them, thousands of years after they had been stoppered up and placed there. There were game boards for games like our checkers or chess. And there were tiny clay statues of servants to wait on the souls just as the servants had waited on them in life.

The tomb chamber of Queen Hatepheres, the mother of the Pharaoh Cheops, was located at the bottom of a hidden ninety-nine-foot shaft near to her son's tomb, the Great Pyramid at Gizeh. In it were the queen's golden razors and manicure set, her armchairs and bed sheathed in gold leaf, the traveling chair in which she had been carried by her servants when she went on a journey. There was a collapsible traveling bedchamber, its framework covered with gold leaf, and a gold curtain box containing fine linen curtains that were hung from the framework to give the queen privacy and keep out mosquitoes.

This is the only royal tomb of the early Old Kingdom time in Egypt that was found undisturbed. In spite of all precautions, most tombs were broken into and stripped of their treasures by grave robbers. Archeologists believe that Hatepheres's original grave was broken into, because the carved stone sarcophagus that should have held the mummy in its case was empty. They think that Cheops had a second tomb dug for his mother, close to his own, but deep under the ground so that it would be safe.

Nearly a thousand years later the capital of Egypt was moved from Memphis to Thebes. Outside of Thebes, in granite cliffs lining what has come to be called the Valley of the Tombs of the Kings, the Pharaohs and government ministers prepared their eternal homes. They had deep passages cut in the cliffs and splendid rooms hollowed out of the solid rock.

All but one of these New Kingdom tombs had been broken open and robbed by the time archeologists discovered them. The one that was found intact, with all its golden furniture and beautiful objects and the body of its owner—in a carved and painted mummy case—undisturbed, was the tomb of the Pharaoh Tut-ankh-amen, who died when he was eighteen. The tomb's entrance was so well hidden within the entrance to another tomb that grave robbers had never found it. It was discovered by the archeologist Howard Carter in 1922—three thousand, two hundred seventy-seven years after Tut-ankh-amen was buried. By coincidence, all the leading members of Carter's expedition died shortly after they had made their sensational discovery and much was made of the supposed Curse of Tut-ankh-amen, a revival of the old superstition that anyone who disturbed a grave would lose his life in punishment.

The treasures of Tut-ankh-amen were sent on tour from the museum in Cairo in 1975, and were seen by millions of people in America and Europe.

Even though the other tombs that have been found in the Valley of the Tombs were stripped of their treasures, they still have much to tell us about the life of royal personages and court officers in ancient Egypt. Along the inner walls of the tomb chambers, painted on the stone in bright life-like colors, there are pictures of all the pleasant things that the people buried there did when they were alive. These wall paintings describe in the liveliest way how the rich Egyptians lived and worked. A royal engineer is shown with his surveyors laying out the site for a building. A royal treasurer is supervising the counting of sheaves of grain paid in as taxes.

In one painting a royal official and his wife and children are eating supper in a leafy arbor in his garden. In another, he is looking over his fields where the farmers are harvesting the grain, and in a corner of the field two farm girls are having a hair-pulling fight. Another picture shows the official and his lady in a boat among the tall

reeds where wild ducks and other water fowl are hiding. He is throwing a net to catch one of them, while she
holds his ankles to keep him from falling out of the slender little boat.

Still another painting shows the lord and lady giving a
dinner party. There are platters of food, jugs of wine
and flowers on the tables. The guests are splendidly
dressed, with jewels and curled wigs. Under the host's
chair the family cat sits waiting for tidbits from the feast,
and in another corner one of the lady guests, who has apparently had too much to eat or drink, is being sick over
a basin.

From these wall paintings in the tombs, and from the
carved and gilded furniture, the jewelry and cosmetics,
the carved ivory boxes and little stone jars and bottles, we
can see that the Egyptians had become very advanced in
the arts and refinements of living. They were also very
skilled in medicine, and Egyptian doctors were considered
the best in the world of that time. And we need only look
at the pyramids to know that they were masters of mathe-
matics, engineering and construction.

Building the Pyramids _____

Across the Nile from Cairo, near the place where ancient
Memphis used to be, are the three great pyramids, which
tourists have traveled to Egypt to see since before the time
of Julius Caesar. The pyramids are huge man-made moun-

tains of gigantic stone blocks. They are the tombs of three
Pharaohs who, more than forty-five hundred years ago,
built them to stand forever as houses for their souls.

The pyramids were built without any of our modern
machinery. We marvel at how the Egyptian workmen and
engineers managed to cut, haul and lift into place such
great blocks of stone weighing many tons apiece, and to
fit them together so expertly. Some of the stone was
quarried across the river. It had to be brought to the river
on sledges, piled on barges and ferried across, then
dragged on sledges from the riverbank to the site where
the pyramid was being built. Each stone was fitted exactly
to the stone beside it in the row, and each row slanted
back from the row below to make the sides of the pyramid slope evenly from the wide base to the point at the
top. As the rows or courses of the stone blocks went
higher and higher, ramps were built along the walls, sloping roadways of broken stone and hard-packed sand. The
next blocks were hauled up these ramps and then were
lifted and levered into place.

The Great Pyramid, the largest of the three near Cairo,
was built for the Pharaoh Cheops. The man who built it
for Cheops was his cousin Hemon, the royal architect and
engineer. A statue of Hemon shows us how he looked, a
strongly built man with an expression of power and in-
telligence. The Great Pyramid is made up of more than
two million great blocks of limestone, and some of the
blocks weigh more than fifteen tons each. After the whole
pyramid was built, it was finished with an outside casing
of finer limestone blocks, all carefully fitted and polished.

This outer covering was probably put in place from the top down, and the ramps would have been taken down bit by bit as the workmen worked their way back to the bottom. There may have been four ramps, one going up from each corner of the pyramid. Three of them could have been used for hauling the heavy blocks up to their places, and the fourth for the workmen coming down with their empty sledges for the next load.

We can imagine the scene under the hot desert sun, with teams of workmen dragging the sledges, one behind the other, up the long slopes, and more teams bending over the stone blocks with ropes and levers. About twenty-five hundred men probably worked at the building itself, and thousands more were cutting and hauling stone from the quarries. The stonecutters used copper saws to cut the limestone blocks out of the quarry and copper chisels to trim them to shape. Limestone is not as hard a rock as some others such as granite, but copper is a very soft metal and cannot be ground to a sharp, hard cutting edge like steel. Yet with such tools the Egyptian stonemasons managed to cut and shape the blocks so exactly that after thousands of years they still fit together without the width of a finger between them.

All this took thousands of workmen, and the work on a single pyramid continued for ten or twenty years. The workmen lived in camps and were well fed and well cared for according to the standards of the time. There are lists of food brought to the camps, including astonishing quantities of onions. There are also references to doctors. The work was hard and dangerous, and there must have been

accidents. The workmen were drafted from all over Egypt,
usually during the flood season when water covered the
fields and there was no farmwork to be done, and they
served for three months at a time.

The first pyramid was not one of the three at Gizeh near
Cairo, but was some distance away at Saqqara. Its builder
was the first man other than a Pharaoh whose name has
come down from those earliest centuries of Egyptian history. He was Imhotep, a physician and scientist as well
as an architect, and he built the pyramid for the Pharaoh
Zoser. What is especially interesting about Imhotep's building is that it shows us how a Pharaoh's palace was built.

The Great House of the Pharaoh was not built of stone.
It was made of woven river reeds and mud plaster and
palm thatch. Its roof was held up by posts made of bun-
dled stalks of papyrus, a tall reed that grows everywhere
along the Nile. Such buildings could not last, and archeologists have never found the remains of a Pharaoh's
palace. But from Imhotep's pyramid we know how it must
have looked.

For the Pharaoh's eternal home Imhotep had every de-
tail of the palace imitated in stone. He had the workmen
carve the garden fence as though it were made of inter-
woven reeds, the house wall as though it had been built
of reeds and plastered over with mud that was smoothed
as it dried. Imhotep imitated the inside of the palace by
lining the walls of one of the rooms in his pyramid with
beautiful blue tiles that looked like the blue-dyed matting
of woven reeds which covered the palace's rough mud-
plastered walls. A thousand years later, the Egyptians

were still following this custom of imitation in stone. When the temple of Karnak was built at the new capital of Thebes, the giant stone pillars there were carved to look like bundles of papyrus stalks, with the flowers of the papyrus in stone at the top.

Land of Peace and Plenty _____

The Egyptians lived under the rule of their Pharaohs for three thousand years, and for most of that time they lived in peace. No other country has ever had such a long peaceful history. From time to time tribes from the highlands of the Sudan in the south would come across the border to raid, and once the Hyksos, or Shepherd Kings, the only successful invaders, ruled for about two hundred years, until a leader arose among the Egyptians who drove them out. This happened at about the middle of Egypt's long history. Afterward a family of warrior kings led Egyptian armies out across the eastern desert and conquered the smaller countries around the eastern shore of the Mediterranean. These small subject countries paid taxes or tribute to the Pharaohs, and expected the Pharaoh's armies to protect them from other invaders. But for the most part they remained free to go on living in their own way, following their own religions and customs and doing business as they had always done.

The Pharaohs did not make alliances with other countries and they very rarely married princesses from other countries. The Pharaohs did not even marry girls out of the noble Egyptian families. They married their own sisters or sometimes their daughters, to keep the power in the family but also for religious reasons. Only one or two of the warrior kings surprised the world of that time by taking a foreign wife.

Throughout Egypt's history the Pharaohs had been men. But one of the warrior kings had a strong-minded and capable daughter named Hatshepsut. When her father died, her husband, who was also her half-brother, was supposed to become the Pharaoh, and her stepson, who was also her nephew, was in line to succeed her husband. But she did not let either of them rule. She had herself declared the Pharaoh, the son of the sun god, and when she appeared in public she dressed like a man in the Pharaoh's robes and wore a false beard.

Queen Hatshepsut ruled Egypt for twenty-two years. Unlike her father, or her nephew who finally succeeded her, she did not lead armies out in campaigns of conquest. She was more interested in trade. She had a fleet of ships built out of Lebanese cedar to sail down the Red Sea coast to a land called Punt, probably on the east coast of Africa, where her captains traded for gold, ivory, ebony, tropical trees and plants for her garden, and dwarfs to amuse her court. The dwarfs are thought to have been pygmy bushmen captured in the heart of Africa.

Hatshepsut built a beautiful temple on the Nile which is still standing, and on its wall there is a painting that tells the story of one of these expeditions. The picture shows her captains exchanging gifts with the tall black

African chief, and beside the chief stands his enormously
fat wife.

It was the custom in those days for each Pharaoh to
have a life-size funeral painting on the wall of the temple
at Karnak, showing himself meeting the gods of the underworld after death. It was also customary to erect an
obelisk in the temple courtyard. The four sides of this
monument were carved with a record of the Pharaoh's
reign and his accomplishments. Hatshepsut put up two
obelisks, the tallest ones in the temple, and she had them
covered from top to bottom with a sheath of gold. The
gold sheathing disappeared long ago, and a later Pharaoh
carved some of his own boasts on one of her obelisks, but
the story of her busy, peaceful reign is still there to be
read.

The Pharaohs were powerful rulers, but sometimes
even a Pharaoh was overthrown by plots in his own palace among captains and ministers he himself had appointed. When this happened, or when a Pharaoh died
without an heir, a new line of Pharaohs, or dynasty, would
come into power. There were thirty dynasties in Egyptian
history. One Pharaoh left a warning to his son who was to
become Pharaoh after him. He had been a good ruler, he
said, and his trusted ministers had turned against him.
He warned his son to be a hard-hearted ruler and not to
trust anyone. In a papyrus scroll that has come down to
our time, he wrote, "Know not a friend. When thou
sleepest, guard for thyself thine own heart, for a man hath
no friend in the day of evil."

The politics that went on in the palace did not much trouble the ordinary people. Egypt, at least for the well-to-do, was a land of peace and plenty. They had time to make and enjoy beautiful objects, to marry and raise their families, to sing and dance and play music on flutes, oboes, cymbals and lutes. But one Pharaoh created a revolution, and because it was a religious revolution it spread dissension among the people.

The Strong Pharaoh

This Pharaoh came to the throne as a youth. He was named Amenhotep IV, after his father and two ancestors. But he changed his name because it honored Egypt's principal god, Amon, and he moved the royal capital from Thebes because that city was sacred to Amon. He abolished all worship of Amon and the many other gods of Egypt, and declared that there was only one god, Aton, the sun, from whom came all light and life. He took the name Ikhnaton for himself and named his capital Akhetaton, Aton's city. He ordered the name of Amon erased from all monuments.

Ikhnaton had his way during the seventeen years of his reign. But when he died the powerful priests of Amon, apparently with strong public feeling behind them, retaliated by destroying Akhetaton and all its monuments.

Fortunately, the destruction was not complete. The ruined city has been excavated at a place called Tel-el-Amarna, and many of the shattered monuments have

been pieced together. Ikhnaton inspired religious literature (hymns to Aton have been rediscovered that are out-
standingly beautiful), and he encouraged an entire school
of art that portrayed people—even royalty—as they really
looked, instead of in the stiff, formal style that was used
before and after his time.

Portrait sculptures show Ikhnaton with his queen Nefertiti and their children in natural, affectionate scenes.
Ikhnaton himself is shown as having been far from handsome, with a long thin face, narrow, sloping shoulders,
thin arms and legs and a sagging abdomen. But Nefertiti,
with her delicate features, her shapely head poised on a
slender neck and her slim, graceful body, must have been
one of history's great beauties. A finished sculpture of her
head, another unfinished one, and many other fascinat-
ing fragments were found at Tel-el-Amarna in what had
been the royal artists' workshop.

Ikhnaton's belief in a single god, the first monotheistic
religion recorded in history, has led some scholars to an
interesting speculation. They point out that although the
Old Testament establishes God as the only deity, the
Bible was written many centuries after the events it de-
scribes actually occurred; and although much of it is
historical, the Bible is regarded as tradition, not history.
These scholars suggest that Moses may have taken the
belief in one God from Ikhnaton. Moses arose to lead the
Israelites out of their bondage in Egypt at least a hundred
years after Ikhnaton's reign. But the Bible tells us that
Moses was rescued and adopted as a baby by an Egyptian
princess and brought up in her palace. The name Moses

is Egyptian. So it is possible, these scholars believe, that Ikhnaton's monotheism was not entirely wiped out by the priests after his death, but lingered on to be revived by the Hebrew leader Moses.

Changing Times _____

In Egypt a thousand years could go by without much change, but eventually change did come. Merchants traveled from other countries to sell lumber, olive oil and other things that Egyptians lacked, and to buy the fine Egyptian jewelry, cosmetics and perfumes. The merchants also brought in new ideas. The Egyptians learned that in other countries people built their houses out of bricks made of mud and straw, hardened in the sun or baked hard in ovens. And so the later houses of wealthy Egyptians were built of bricks like these, and had flat roofs on which the family could sit to enjoy the breeze from the river in the evenings.

The Egyptians invented their own picture writing, which we call hieroglyphics, and continued to use it long after other people had developed the alphabet. They may also have invented a simpler writing form, which we call demotic, or they may have learned it from foreign merchants who were already using it to keep their accounts. Writing was first invented by the Sumerians even before the Pharaoh Menes brought the two Egypts under one government.

When they began to write, the Egyptians found a new use for their papyrus reeds. By hammering out the papyrus stalks into thin flat strips, then pressing the strips together at their edges to make sheets, they made a material on which they could write. Then they sharpened the end of a bird's quill to make a pen, and mixed water with soot from the fireplace or any dark vegetable juice to make ink. We make our writing sheets out of rags or wood pulp, using a method the Chinese invented and the Western world learned about long afterward. But *paper,* the word that comes from *papyrus,* is still the name we give these sheets.

Quite a lot of Egyptian historical, religious and medical literature, as well as poetry, has been found, written on papyrus rolls and stored in the tombs, sometimes tucked within the wrappings of a mummy. Here is an Egyptian love poem that has come down to us over the space of thousands of years. From the feeling it expresses it might have been written yesterday. It was written by an Egyptian woman.

> I am thy first sister,
> And thou art to me as the garden
> Which I have planted with flowers
> And all sweet-smelling herbs . . .
> The beautiful place where we walk
> When thy hand rests within mine,
> With thoughtful mind and joyous heart
> Because we walk together.
> It is intoxicating to me to hear thy voice,

And my life depends upon hearing thee.
Whenever I see thee,
It is better for me than food or drink.

The long story of Egypt came to an end about two thousand years ago, and by that time the pyramids were already older than the monuments of Greece and Rome are to us today. The young Macedonian king, Alexander the Great, conquered Egypt, founded Alexandria, a new city on the Egyptian coast named for himself, and declared himself the Pharaoh. In the temple of Karnak, where the funeral paintings of all the Pharaohs were placed, Alexander added his funeral painting too. In the painted and sculptured picture he stands in the ancient style of the Pharaohs, meeting the gods and becoming one of them. He is wearing the same royal costume as the other Pharaohs, and the gods are the same—the hawk-headed god, the goddess with the head of a lioness, and all the other strange-looking gods of ancient Egypt. But instead of the royal Egyptian head with the royal wig and beard, his portrait has the boyish head familiar from Greek statues, with short curly hair and no beard.

Alexander did not stay to rule as Pharaoh of Egypt. He went on to other conquests in India and Persia, where he died at the age of thirty-three. But he left Ptolemy, one of his generals, to begin a new Greek line of Pharaohs.

The Ptolemies ruled in the Greek manner. Alexandria became their capital. With the Greek love of learning, they built a library and university there, and the city became a center of science and scholarship for the whole ancient world.

The last of the Ptolemies was Cleopatra, a famous beauty and the second woman to rule Egypt. When Egypt was conquered by the Romans, Cleopatra killed herself by putting a poisonous snake to her breast rather than be taken as a captive to Rome. And so, after three thousand years, the ancient Egyptian era came to an end.

Part 4

People of the Bible

Between the great kingdoms of Egypt on the west and Mesopotamia on the east lay the crescent-shaped Mediterranean shore, the land of the Bible. Mountains rose up behind the shore in broken ranges, with grassy highland plateaus. Little rivers, mere streams compared with the Nile or the twin rivers of Mesopotamia, ran down from the mountains to the sea. Large and small islands dotted the nearby waters of the sea.

It was a green, well-watered land—as the Bible says and the archeologists confirm, a land of milk and honey. An Egyptian traveler named Sinuhe, who lived with a wandering tribe and married one of the tribeswomen, wrote of his adventures when he returned to Egypt. This is how he described the land of the Bible as it was in his time, four thousand years ago: "Figs there were in it and grapes. It had more wine than water. Plentiful its honey, abundant its olives. Its trees bore every fruit. Barley was there and wheat. There was no limit to the kind of cattle."

This land was very different from the broad plain of Mesopotamia or the long valley and wide delta of Egypt. It was so broken up in varied shapes that it gave living space to many different peoples with different ways of life. Mountain folk tended their herds and flocks in the highlands. Farmers cultivated their fields in the river valleys and along the shore of the Mediterranean. Where the shore was too narrow and rocky for farming, the people became seafarers and made their living by fishing and by trade.

The people along the shore, and those who lived inland in the highlands and river valleys, all formed separate nations, each different from its neighbors in language, customs and beliefs. Every now and then an ambitious ruler from Egypt or Mesopotamia or from one of the rising kingdoms in the north sent in his army to conquer them and make them pay tribute. But even when they were conquered by a foreign ruler, these Mediterranean nations managed to preserve their own ways of life. Frequently, when the Egyptian and Mesopotamian kingdoms were too busy with internal affairs to bother with conquest, the Mediterranean nations achieved complete independence.

Each nation was a small kingdom with its own king, or a group of tribes with their chieftain, and each had its own gods and goddesses. But they met and mingled, too, in war as fellow captives or soldiers in the armies of the great kings, and through trading in peacetime. They intermarried, sometimes kidnaping and sometimes buying brides from each other. These little nations were never united into a single people, but they learned from each other. They exchanged crafts and inventions, fashions in jewelry, religious customs, and made this part of the world of five thousand years ago a melting pot of peoples.

Not all these nations in the middle land were small and powerless. From time to time, one of them rose to considerable importance in the ancient world, only to decline and vanish from history. One such nation, unearthed as recently as 1975 in what is now Syria, had almost two hundred and sixty thousand inhabitants—a strikingly large population for that time—with a capital city of almost twenty thousand people, eleven thousand of them employed as government administrators or civil servants. This country, called Ebla, rose from a small tributary colony of Sumer to become an independent kingdom which thrived for about eight hundred years, doing business with the farming communities around it and with the powerful kingdoms of Egypt, Sumer and Akkad.

The Italian archeologists who discovered the capital city uncovered grand stairways decorated with inlaid shells, carved wooden animals, decorated furniture, sculptures in wood, stone and metal. They also excavated a room of the royal palace where they found the palace archives. The room had been lined with wooden shelves, but the wood had decayed and some fifteen thousand clay tablets that had once been lined up along the shelves had fallen to the floor. The tablets were inscribed in the cuneiform writing of Mesopotamia, but in a Semitic language unknown until the time of the Italian discovery. Fortunately, a dictionary—actually a group of tablets—was also found. The dictionary gave Sumerian definitions for the words in the newly discovered language and from those definitions, the archeologists could read the Eblaite tablets. The archives dealt with matters of government and trade: international treaties, military campaigns, textile manufacturing and metal-working industries run by the government. There was also an account of a wedding. The daughter of a king of Ebla married the king of a Meso-

potamian city-state, and the groom received several Eb-
lan towns as a wedding gift.

This middle land along the Mediterranean coast was
also a crossroads where many wandering peoples met,
especially the two great branches of the human family,
the Semites and the Indo-Europeans. The settled, prosperous lands attracted the wandering peoples, who were
generally poor. They came from the Arabian deserts in
the south, across the mountains from the east and down
from the highlands and mountains in the north. Sometimes they came by sea, across the Mediterranean. Although no one really knows where the sea people came
from, some historians believe they were wilderness people from Europe.

Sometimes the newcomers overran the settled people,
mingled with them and became absorbed by them. Sometimes they drove out the inhabitants, who in turn became
wanderers. Occasionally, a wave of wanderers pushing
from behind drove waves of other people ahead of them.
The wave might come in the form of a conquering army
or a horde of killing and looting tribesmen. But most of
the time the newcomers came in small groups over hundreds of years.

One large family of wanderers were the Semites, who
probably came from Arabia and migrated into Mesopotamia. These were the Semitic peoples who later became
strong enough to overthrow the Sumerians and establish
their own kingdoms of Babylonia and Assyria.

At this time, about four thousand years ago, the Semitic
newcomers were herdsmen and shepherds, pasturing

their flocks outside the Sumerian cities and living in their own quarter of the city. They were the caravan masters of the inland trade, men who knew the desert routes. Each year they set out with trains of pack asses, carrying gold, ivory, precious stones and fine fabrics, the luxury goods that came to Sumer across the Persian Gulf. They traveled across the western desert, sold their goods in the crossroads cities and the Mediterranean ports, and came back with silver and marble from the north, linen from Egypt, cedar from Lebanon. One of these colonies of herdsmen-traders was in the city of Mari, north of Ur on the bank of the Euphrates River. According to the royal records written on clay tablets that have been found there, among the Semitic tribesmen in Mari was a group called the Habiru. The Egyptians also mentioned the Habiru in papyrus records of that time. This may have been the ancient name of the Hebrews.

The Hebrew People

Long afterward, when the Hebrews had established a kingdom of their own in Palestine, they dated their history from those beginnings in Mesopotamia. They told the story of Terah, who took his family out of Ur and moved to Canaan, as Palestine was then called. In the history of Ur, that was a time of political troubles, and probably a good time for outsiders like the Semitic caravan masters to go elsewhere.

Terah's tribe was a group of many families, perhaps

three or four hundred people, all related to one another by blood and marriage. They had large flocks of sheep and goats and several hundred pack asses to carry their possessions. The old people and young children rode in four-wheeled carts drawn by bullocks; the others went on foot.

In Haran, after a two months' journey covering about six hundred fifty miles, they rested. Haran was a busy commercial city on the caravan route that led through Canaan to Egypt. Terah died in Haran, and Abraham, his eldest son and now head of the family, took up the journey again. Caravans carrying trade goods turned off along the way to the thriving coastal towns of Tyre, Ugarit, and Byblos on the eastern Mediterranean shore. But Abraham, leading a tribe with all its women and children, flocks and possessions, followed the inland route through fertile Canaan where their flocks and pack animals found pasture. Near a small fortified town, called Bethel in the Bible, Abraham built an altar and camped. An ancient altar has been found there, with traces of sacrificial fires still remaining after thousands of years.

Abraham's people were one of many wandering tribes on the inland plains and deserts. Such a tribe lived in tents of animal skins, followed its flocks from pasture to pasture, kept to its own customs and religions. When one of the periodic droughts burned the plains and there was no forage for the animals, the tribe might make its way to Egypt. A wall painting in the tomb of an Egyptian nobleman who lived about four thousand years ago, at the eastern edge of the Nile delta near the desert, shows the arrival of such a group of nomads, whom the Egyptians called "sand dwellers."

The painting shows us how the "sand dwellers" looked. In the painting they are dressed in colorful patterned clothes unlike the pure white of the Egyptians. The men are in kilts with bare torsos from the waist up, the women in shifts with one shoulder bare, their long black hair hanging loose below a narrow headband. The men are wearing sandals, the women have anklets but walk barefoot and the young children ride two by two in the pack saddles of the donkeys. Their weapons are bows, throwing sticks, spears. One of the men carries a harp, and a bellows and an anvil are strapped to the donkeys, telling us that the desert folk were musicians and coppersmiths. They are shown bringing gifts to the nobleman, whose permission they must have to camp on his land.

Abraham's people were nomads like those in the painting. According to the Bible, their stay in the Nile valley was prosperous. When Abraham left Egypt, the Bible says, he was very rich in cattle, gold and silver.

There came a time when a line of warrior Pharaohs sent their armies as far north as Syria, conquering the independent small kingdoms in their path. The Pharaohs exacted tribute from the rich cities, but the nomads were usually poor and could not pay. The Egyptians took many of them into slavery. This was the time of bondage described in the Bible, when the Israelites, as they then called themselves, were forced into slavery along with thousands of others and were set to work for the Pharaoh.

The Pharaoh whom Moses challenged was Ramses II,

a famous builder who erected the great temples at Karnak and Thebes and the rock temple at Abu-Simbel. The Pharaoh's treasure cities in the land of Goshen, where the Israelite slaves lived, have been excavated. Goshen was in the eastern part of the Nile delta, a district of lush gardens, orchards and waters full of fish.

Moses led a great insurrection of the Israelite slaves and they escaped into the Sinai peninsula, where they returned to the old nomadic life. After a time of desert wandering they set out under their warrior leader Joshua to win a land of their own. The archeologists have traced the path of Joshua's conquests, and have found some of the towns that fell to his assault. One of them, Gibeon, had a tunnel by which the inhabitants could steal out at night to get water when the town was under siege. Another, the ancient walled town of Jericho, shows evidence of once having been burned down. According to the custom of the time, a conqueror killed the inhabitants and burned the town.

Near a Canaanite town called Megiddo (Armageddon in the Bible), on the plain of Esdraelon, a battlefield has been excavated that shows the debris of many ancient armies. Syrians, Egyptians, Canaanites and Israelites fought there. A picture inlaid on ivory, found at Megiddo and dating from the time of the Israelite invasion of Canaan, shows two prisoners of war, bearded and naked except for their turban-like helmets, being led by a foot soldier and a charioteer before a Canaanite king. This may have recorded a battle that the Israelites lost. But eventually they fought their way to the region west of the Jordan River and established a kingdom of their own.

Like the other small nations around them, the Hebrew people kept their own ways. Their religion was a strange one for that time. The people living around them worshiped many different gods and goddesses and made images to which they prayed in their temples. But the Hebrew people worshiped only one God, whom they called Jehovah, and they made no images of Him. They believed He was everywhere, and could not be seen or pictured.

They also had some laws that were special to them. They were not allowed to eat certain foods. Today we suspect that these were really health laws, because the foods that were forbidden spoil quickly, especially in a hot climate, and they often carry disease. Shellfish, for example, can carry the bacteria that cause ptomaine poisoning.

The Israelite people were often tempted to follow the worship of their neighbors. It was not easy to worship an unseen God when their neighbors had splendid golden idols to say their prayers to. But when they strayed away from their own God and their laws, their leaders warned them that Jehovah would punish them with troubles at home or invading armies from abroad. And of course, like the other small nations around them, they were often attacked and sometimes conquered. For many years after they had settled in their land, they had to fight to keep it.

Kings in Israel _____

The Israelites had three great rulers. The first was Saul, an able general who defended the country against their most powerful neighbors, the Philistines. A few miles north of Jerusalem the remains of a walled and turreted citadel have been found; it dates from King Saul's time of about three thousand years ago and is thought to have been Saul's castle.

Saul was killed in battle, and his successor was David, the shepherd boy who, in the Bible story, killed the Philistine leader Goliath with his slingshot. David brought the twelve tribes of the Israelites into a single nation, with Jerusalem as its capital. It is since the time of King David that Jerusalem has been considered a holy city, first for the Jews and later also for the Christians and the Mohammedans. David was a musician and a poet, and most of the Psalms in the Bible are his poems.

David's son Solomon was a poet like his father, and he was also a wise man and a philosopher. The Bible's great love poem, the Song of Songs, and many of the wise sayings in the books of Proverbs and Ecclesiastes in the Bible are thought to have been written by Solomon.

Solomon was a worldly man and a practical ruler. His name means "peaceful," from the Hebrew word *shalom*, meaning "peace." Solomon did not waste his little country's wealth in wars or battles about boundaries with his neighbors. Instead he took advantage of its location and developed peaceful trade.

The Jordan River valley was rich and fertile, and the

country had farm products to trade. The people could sell grain, fruits and vegetables, palm and olive oils, honey and beeswax. Solomon also developed a sea trade, one of his most imaginative ventures. His people, descendants of the "sand dwellers," had no experience with the sea, and his country was almost landlocked. Far to the south, at the end of the long desert called the Negev, was a small bay, the Gulf of 'Aqaba, that led to the Red Sea, and from there to the Arabian Sea and the Indian Ocean.

Solomon's nearest neighbor was King Hiram of Tyre, from whom he had bought Lebanon cedar and hired Phoenician builders to build his palace and his splendid temple in Jerusalem. Hiram's people were great sailors and shipbuilders, and so Solomon made a treaty with Hiram to build a fleet at Solomon's small port, Ezion-geber, on the Gulf of 'Aqaba that opened into the eastern seas. The fleet of merchant ships, built there by Hiram's shipbuilders and manned by his Phoenician sailors, traded up and down the east coast of Arabia and Africa, along the Persian Gulf and possibly even to the coast of India.

The two kings reaped a fortune in this joint enterprise. Their ships brought back elephant ivory, precious stones and metals, and monkeys and beautiful tropical birds to amuse the wives of kings and rich men in their harem gardens. The markets of Jerusalem and Tyre became famous in the world of three thousand years ago.

According to the Bible, this fleet of merchant ships brought Solomon more than thirteen tons of gold on its first voyage, and later, in the course of a single year, brought another twenty-one tons. Solomon had so much gold that when he built the temple in Jerusalem, he had not only the altar and the doors covered with gold but the walls and floors as well. In his palace he had his ivory throne overlaid with gold. Scholars estimate that Solomon possessed about half of all the gold mined in the world at that time.

The source of all this gold, a place called Ophir in the Bible, was for many centuries one of the mysteries of archeology. Quite recently a team of American and Saudi-Arabian scientists announced their discovery of what they are certain was Solomon's gold mine. It is at a place called Madh adh Dhahab, meaning "cradle of gold," on an ancient trade route between Arabia and Solomon's seaport at 'Aqaba. It would have been easy for porters and pack animals to transport the gold to the coast, a distance of 149 miles, and from there, the 372 miles by sea to 'Aqaba. The slopes of the mine are littered with stone hammers and grindstones used by the workers to crush the ore and extract the particles of precious metal.

Solomon's other great enterprise was the mining of copper, the most valuable trading item of the time. His mines were located at the southern tip of the Negev desert. Archeologists have found there, not only the traces of his ancient seaport, but the miners' dwellings, the mine galleries and the smelting furnaces. And they discovered that Solomon's engineers had ingeniously placed the smelting furnaces in a direct line with the deep rift valley so that their fires were continually fanned by the desert winds that blow there night and day.

Nothing has been found of Solomon's splendid palace

where, in the Bible story, the beautiful Queen of Sheba
visited him, having come all the way from Ethiopia to see
whether the stories of his wealth and wisdom were true.
Considering the value of the products that were coming
from her land and others in Africa, and the taxes that
Solomon's customs officers were collecting on those products as they came through Ezion-geber, historians suggest
that she probably came to negotiate a trade agreement.

Solomon's temple was built by Phoenician builders and
decorated by Phoenician craftsmen, the best in the world
at that time. It was adorned inside and out with carvings,
gold and silver inlays, ivory and mother-of-pearl, and was
hung with silks and fine fabrics. It is said that hundreds
of musicians played there on the high holidays. In the
centuries after Solomon's time the temple was destroyed
and rebuilt several times. Only one part of its western
wall remains, as part of the Wailing Wall in Jerusalem.

The Phoenicians

King Solomon's allies and trading partners, the Phoenicians, formed another branch of the Semitic family of
peoples. Long before the Israelites came to Palestine,
these Semites had settled on the shore of the eastern
Mediterranean, in a narrow strip about a hundred miles
long and ten miles wide between the mountains and the
sea. Their land, called Lebanon, was too narrow for much
farming, but the mountains that rose up behind them
on the land side were green with forests of cedar, and

this became their first valuable trade item. The city of Byblos, the first of the trading cities of this land, sold cedar to a Pharaoh of Egypt to build ships about forty-seven hundred years ago. Cheops, who built the first of the three great pyramids, bought cedar from Byblos for the funeral boat that carried his body across the Nile to his pyramid when he died. The boat was found about twenty years ago, carefully buried near the pyramid, and the cedar out of which it was made was still faintly fragrant.

The fame of the cedar of Lebanon spread to Mesopotamia as well, and caravans from Sumer came across the mountains to buy lumber for King Gudea in Lagash. The merchants of the Phoenician coast cities also sold wine from their hillside vineyards, pitch from the resin of their trees, wax and olive oil. Phoenician craftsmen became good metalworkers, and they produced copper tools, silver bowls, gold clasps for belts and cloaks. Their merchants brought back elephant ivory from Africa, and the Phoenicians became famous throughout the ancient world for their carved ivory boxes, beads, amulets and seals.

The Phoenicians were also excellent weavers and dyers, and their merchants sold the cloth and, separately, the dye, called Tyrian purple. On the shore beside the ancient harbor of Sidon, another of their cities, there is still a mound of seashells more than twice as high as a person. They are the shells of the murex, a small shellfish from which the Phoenicians made their purple dye.

The Phoenicians' great talent was that they could do

business with anyone anywhere. They had no territory except their narrow strip of land between the mountains and the sea. They had no armies, no generals in armor riding swift chariots, no ruler and, in fact, no nation. Theirs is a history of separate cities. Each city consisted of a harbor full of ships, crowded little streets around the harbor filled with craftsmen of all kinds, and a huge market, or bazaar, where goods from all over the world were traded. There was a temple to the city's protective god, and a palace for the city's king. But the wealth of the city was in its shipping, and the life of the city was in its bazaars.

Sidon was the second of the Phoenician trading cities, and Tyre was the third. Most of Tyre, including King Hiram's palace, the temple and the great bazaar, was on a little island just off the shore. The temple of Tyre that inspired Solomon to build one like it in Jerusalem was a whole compound of buildings, large and small, gleaming with decorations in ivory and precious metals. Ships and boats of all nations lay at anchor in Tyre's harbor, and goods from everywhere came by boat and by caravan to its market fairs. Wool and woven woolen goods, grains, raw metals, tools, jewelry, carved wooden chests filled with silks or spices, fat sheep, cattle and swine, horses from the northern plains, mountain donkeys and desert camels were brought to the bazaar in Tyre.

The work of the Phoenician craftsmen has been found in all the cities of the ancient world, from Mesopotamia to Italy and Spain. In Italy, long before the beginning of Rome, there lived a people called the Etruscans, who may

originally have migrated to Italy from Lydia on the eastern Mediterranean shore. The Etruscan noblemen had
their fine wares made for them in Tyre, and the Phoenician craftsmen gave them the most fashionable designs
of the time.

One Etruscan prince had a silver bowl engraved with
a picture story that showed him driving out in his chariot
for a day's hunting and being attacked by some strange
hairy monsters that look like gorillas. Gorillas were never
seen in Italy or in Tyre, but some Phoenician merchants
who had traveled to Africa had described them at home,
and the monsters engraved on the bowl were the Phoenician silversmith's idea of how gorillas must look. The
picture story went on to show the Etruscan prince being
rescued from the gorillas by the Phoenician goddess As-
tarte. The whole design is in the style of Assyria which,
as the most powerful empire in the ancient world at that
time, led the fashion.

The Phoenician craftsmen cleverly imitated all the
styles of the times, but they always had a touch of their
own which archeologists recognize. Even the style of their
ships was distinctive. They are pictured in Egyptian wall
paintings with their high prows and triangular sails,
drawn up on the beach while the merchants present their
trays of fruit and jars of wine and oil to be weighed and
checked off by the Pharaoh's port officials. A Phoenician
ship might carry livestock, perhaps bulls from Syria, or it
might bring an entire cargo of murex shells from which
the Egyptian weavers and dyers, who were also very
skilled, would make the dye for a royal official's cloak.

In the paintings the Phoenician merchant's black curly hair and beard are neatly trimmed and he wears a headband across his forehead. His costume, a length of fringed and bordered cloth wound around his body from knees to armpits, ends in a short cape over his shoulders. The Egyptian painting also shows Phoenician women wearing long white dresses with rows of flounces from shoulder to hem. Their long black hair hangs loose down their backs.

With their arts of shipbuilding and navigation, their fine crafts and their talent for trade, the Phoenicians made themselves so useful in the ancient world that they prospered for about two thousand years. Other peoples appeared and vanished, empires rose and fell, but the Phoenician merchant ships went on, plying up and down the Mediterranean, spreading the wares of civilized living around the known world. And in addition to their varied cargoes, they carried with them one more precious contribution, the alphabet.

The Alphabet

The invention of signs for single letters instead of for whole syllables was developed by the Phoenicians as a part of their busy trade. They dealt with people who spoke many different languages, and they traded in many kinds of items. For this, they needed a more efficient form of writing than the picture syllables of Egyptian hieroglyphics or the cuneiform syllables of old Sumer and later Babylon. Single letters could be combined to make words in almost any language. And so the Phoenician alphabet became the basis for the alphabets of all the ancient peoples of that crowded world, Hebrews, Persians, Greeks and many more who disappeared long ago. When the Romans came along, they adopted the same alphabet for their language, Latin. It is the alphabet, with letters somewhat changed from their ancient forms, that we use in our writing today.

Tyre was conquered time after time, by the Assyrians, the Babylonians, the Persians and finally by Alexander the Great. He had his men fill in the narrow neck of the sea so that his big battering rams and siege towers could be dragged out from the shore to attack the island city's walls. That was the end of Tyre.

But Phoenician ships and sailors continued to sail the Mediterranean, often in the navies of their conquerors. The last great Phoenician city was Carthage, far off to the west on the Mediterranean shore of Africa. Originally it was founded as a colony and trading post by merchants from Tyre, and it survived to become such a serious rival to Rome that Hannibal, a great general from Carthage, led an expedition across the sea to Europe and then over the Alps, to threaten the city of Rome itself. His feat is famous in history, but Rome did not fall and finally its armies destroyed Carthage. Nothing is left now of the last great Phoenician city except the ruins of the Roman army encampment in the desert, Leptis Magna.

Part 5

People of the Indus

Overleaf:
The dramatic end of Mohenjo-Daro in the Indus Valley is imagined in this scene of chariot-riding warriors, probably Aryan nomads from the north, sweeping past the walls of the citadel and giant granaries to destroy the city and its people. The bearded figure is adapted from a soapstone sculpture, one of the few portraits the Indus people left of themselves.

East of Mesopotamia lies the mountainous land of Persia, which we know as Iran—a form of its more ancient name. East of Iran lies a river valley longer and broader than the valley of the Nile or the plains of Mesopotamia's twin rivers. It has been called the Land of the Nine Rivers because a whole system of rivers carries the snows and rains from the Himalaya Mountains in the north into one great river, the Indus, which flows into the Indian Ocean. Part of the Indus River country is now in Pakistan and part is in India.

In the world of five thousand years ago this was the country called Meluhha. Caravans from Mesopotamia came across the Iranian mountains to trade there. Ships from Arabian and Israeli ports on the Red Sea and others from Sumerian and Babylonian ports on the Persian Gulf followed the coast to the Indus River towns. The excellent cotton for cloth, the gold and ivory, the red carnelian and blue lapis lazuli gemstones, the fine teakwood and other rare and precious goods came only from this far-off country. These goods fetched a high price at home and made the long journey worthwhile.

Except for foreign traders, the people of the Indus valley had few dealings with the people beyond the valley's mountainous western border. A governing class of businessmen lived in the comfortable town houses, but most of the population were farmers, and their fathers had been farmers before them, longer than anyone knows.

There were some areas of swamp and jungle where poisonous snakes and dangerous wild beasts lurked, but most of their vast valley was fertile. They raised good crops of wheat, barley and sesame, and they were the first to cultivate cotton. They grew melons and dates, and bred buffaloes, horses, donkeys and camels. Their farm villages stretched for hundreds of miles along the coast and inland along the rivers.

The Indus Valley had two great cities. Mohenjo-Daro, about two hundred miles up the river from the seacoast, ruled the southern part of the land. Harappa, nearly four hundred miles farther up the valley to the northeast, governed the north. The excavations show that they were large cities for that time. It would take a person a good half hour to walk from one end to the other along one of the broad avenues. Unlike Ur and Babylon, which had perhaps one large avenue and a clutter of twisting narrow alleys, the Indus cities were laid out in a plan like a checkerboard, with regular blocks of houses and straight wide streets.

In Mohenjo-Daro, the houses were of whitewashed brick. A windowless outer wall faced the street, and all the rooms opened on an inner courtyard. The streets were unpaved and dusty, but underneath them ran a remarkably modern sewer system of brick drains, with manholes which provided the city sanitation workers access to them.

Looking out over the city from its western side was a brick citadel or fort, about fifty feet high, with watch-towers rising above the walls. Close by were the granaries, huge storehouses for the grain raised on the valley farmlands. The grain, or the flour that was ground from it, was apparently used as the local currency. The farmers brought their sheaves of grain by river boat or oxcart to an outer gate in the citadel wall, and the sheaves were hauled up into storage buildings that were solidly constructed of timber and bricks.

The citadel was the center of both government and religion. On top of the citadel there were pillared halls for meetings or worship, small rooms with hollowed-out baths, probably for the priests, and a huge public bath. The bath as a purification rite was part of the religious observance.

Below the citadel the city spread out to cover an area about three miles in circumference. There were residential areas, shops, public eating places and probably an inn for travelers. When a caravan arrived or was preparing to leave, the streets would teem with farmers, city folk and strange-looking visitors from other lands. The city also had its entertainments. No painting and very little sculpture has been found in its ruins, but archeologists have recovered a charming little bronze figure of a dancing girl, her head tilted back and her thick curly hair tied behind. All she is wearing is an armful of bangles and a necklace with pendants.

The cities of the Indus were apparently built by invading conquerors, and they stood for a thousand years, but we know very little about them. No tablets or inscriptions have been found to tell their history or even the names of their rulers. But we do know the story of how they ended.

The Death of a City _____

The end of Mohenjo-Daro was sudden and bloody. When the ruins were uncovered, archeologists could plainly read the dramatic story of how it perished thirty-five hundred years ago.

The city may already have lost some of its greatness before it was destroyed. Land had been cleared too drastically, floods had become too destructive because all the trees and shrubs had been cut down and as a result the city's wealth had obviously diminished. Its decline is evident from the ruins. New houses were not as well built as the old ones, and trade had fallen off.

There could not have been much warning that invaders were at hand. Most of the population simply fled for their lives into the country or in boats down the river, leaving all their belongings. Of those who stayed, perhaps to save their possessions, some fled down to the city walls and were killed on the steps or in the lane, and others were caught in their houses and killed on the spot. In one house thirteen people, adults and children, lay where they had fallen, and the bones show that each one was probably killed by a single slash of a sword.

Strangely, the raiders did not stop to loot. The bodies still wore bracelets, rings and bead necklaces when the scene of this ancient massacre came to light about fifty years ago. The raiders did not stay to occupy the city or build a new one over the old, as invaders usually did in the past. They simply slaughtered the people they found, and went on.

Up the river in the northeast, Harappa seems to have suffered the same fate, probably some years earlier. That city's ruins were plundered many years afterward for building stone, and so its story is not so easy to decipher.

Neither of the two cities was inhabited again. Both were left forever in silence and solitude, their dead unburied, until the winds covered them with the shifting valley soil. The surrounding farm culture that the cities had governed disappeared almost without a trace.

Who were the attackers? No clue has been found in the cities themselves. If they had settled, something of their culture would have remained, layered above the ruins of the old. Had they been farmers or city dwellers, they would probably have stayed on to take advantage of those already developed cities and fields. The fact that they took the people of the cities by surprise indicates a swift attack. Probably the invaders came in chariots.

The Strangers

A people of this kind did come to northern India at about that time. They were neither farmers nor city dwellers. They were nomads, wandering tribes who herded their cattle on the grassy steppes and plains north of the moun-

tains of Iran and pitched their tents wherever they
stopped for pasture. They had horses which they had
tamed from the wild herds on the Asian plains, and they
rode in chariots and carried their families and household
goods in horse-drawn wagons. They belonged to the Indo-
European branch of the human family, and those tribes
that came into India called themselves Aryan, which in
their language meant "noble."

Their language was Sanskrit. Their holy scriptures, the
Vedas, tell their history in the same way that the Bible
tells the history of the Hebrew tribes of the Semites. Like
the Old Testament of the Bible, the Vedas are filled with
poetry and tales of wonderful happenings. Like the Bible,
the Vedas can be read both for their beauty and inspira-
tion and for clues to the historical facts that may lie behind the marvels.

Like the Hebrews, who were also nomads, the Aryans
did not believe in the earth gods and goddesses, the fertility deities of the farmer. Their gods were sky gods
which we know by their Greek names as the gods of Mount
Olympus and by their later Roman names. The Greeks
were another, later branch of the Indo-European people.
The Greek language, the Latin language of the Romans
and all the languages of modern Europe, including English, are all members of the same language family as
Sanskrit, the language of the Aryans. The actual *letters*
of our alphabet came to us from the Phoenicians, but the
language that we read, write and speak is one of many
branches descended from the speech of the Indo-European nomads of the Asian steppes.

During the centuries after their invasion of India, the Aryans settled down on the land and their religion developed into the peaceful beliefs of Hinduism. But at the beginning, according to the oldest portions of the Vedas, they were a warrior people. Their war god was Indra, and they called him the fort-destroyer. The Vedas tell of great cities and citadels that Indra destroyed. Could these cities have been Harappa and Mohenjo-Daro? These are secrets of the past that we may never decipher.

Part 6

People of the Sea

The island of Crete lies in the middle of the eastern Mediterranean across the route from Greece to Egypt. On the map it has the look of a long slender ship. Crete is a large island, with a shoreline of beaches and deeply indented bays that make good shelter for ships. From the shore, the plains roll gently up to a range of craggy mountains that form the island's spine. The first people to settle there probably came from the delta land of Egypt or else from the eastern Mediterranean shore. They were farmers and fishermen who used stone tools. But they must already have had some knowledge of boat building and sailing, since the only way to reach Crete was by sea.

Some of them sailed farther on to settle on the seaward edges of Greece, some sixty miles or so from the northern shore of Crete. Some went on to the many small islands which lie along the coast, stretching like stepping-stones from Greece to the shore of Asia, where the Asian peninsula of Anatolia reaches toward Europe, separated from it by only a narrow strip of water that we now call the Dardanelles.

About five thousand years ago the farming and fishing villages of Crete began to grow into cities. Pottery and metalcraft developed and merchant ships were built, large galleys with room for as many as thirty or forty rowers and probably one mast that could hold a single sail. The Cretans could sail northeast to the Asian coast for copper from the mountainous Anatolian peninsula, or due east to the Syrian port of Aleppo, where the caravans came overland from Mesopotamia, or south to the delta harbors of Egypt.

As time went on, they sailed farther west—to Italy, Sicily, Sardinia and the shores of Spain—always seeking metals for their craftsmen. They may have dared to sail on, past the great Rock of Gibraltar into the Atlantic, to follow the wild coast of Europe to Brittany and across the dangerous channel waters to Wales and Ireland. They found copper in the rough western lands, then tin, which they blended with the copper to make bronze for the fine daggers and beautiful clasps and buckles that by then had become valuable articles of trade. In Ireland they traded for gold which wild-looking tribesmen in animal skins had gathered from the banks and shallow beds of the Irish streams.

The Cretan people prospered in this trade, and their towns grew into cities. In its great years the island was said to have ninety or a hundred thriving cities. Unlike cities on the mainland, they needed no fortifications because the sea and their fighting ships protected them. Instead of building city walls with sentinel towers and battlements, they built fine stone houses with many rooms for their wealthy merchants and palaces for their princes.

Their palaces, which archeologists have carefully dug out of the earth that covered them for thousands of years, can be seen today. Nothing that has been found out of the ancient past is as splendid as these Cretan ruins. They are like fairy-tale palaces, with broad stairways leading to throne rooms, bed chambers, bathrooms with painted

walls and decorated bathtubs. There are long wide hall-
ways, and all along the walls are painted life-size figures
of elegantly gowned and jeweled court ladies and court
gentlemen walking in processions.

The Painted Ladies ————————————————

On the walls around the grand courtyard are paintings of
ladies in flounced gowns with bare bosoms, sitting as
though in box seats at the theater. In some of the royal
rooms the walls are painted with dolphins, flying fish,
dainty flowers and graceful plants, all in rich bright colors. One of the famous paintings from a palace wall shows
a young lady with makeup on her large lively eyes and
smiling lips. Her hair is curled and piled high under a
large hat.

Another portrait, which archeologists named the Cup-
bearer, shows an aristocratic young gentleman in splendid court costume, carrying a tall, slender blue drinking
cup or goblet. His hair falls in a thick brown braid on his
shoulder, his cloak is of costly embroidered material, and
he is wearing an earring, a necklace, a gold armlet and,
around his narrow waist, a glittering jeweled belt.

These portraits were found on the walls of the palace of
Knossos, the grandest of the Cretan palaces, and are
called frescoes. *Fresco* is an Italian word that means
"fresh." The fresco technique is to paint directly on the
fresh plaster of the wall so that the colors and the design
sink into the plaster while it is wet and become a per-

manent part of it when it dries. Today these paintings seem almost as bright and fresh as when the royal artists of Crete first made them thirty-five hundred years ago.

As they are shown in these paintings, the Cretan people were small, slender and graceful. The men as well as the women took pride in their narrow waists and pulled their wide belts tight. The men wore only a short skirt like a kilt. Their legs and their bodies were bare, a comfortable costume in the hot sunny climate of Crete, and they had long cloaks to throw around their shoulders when it was chilly.

The women wore long dresses with frilly flounces all the way to the ground, and dainty embroidered shoes on their small feet. The bodice of the dress was tiny and fitted snugly, probably stiffened with some kind of corseting. It had short puffed sleeves and stood up in a high collar in back, but in front it was deeply cut out to show the whole bosom. Both the men and the women wore their hair long and elaborately dressed, with braids or long locks hanging down and curls around the face and on the forehead. Both men and women also wore quantities of jewelry, made with precious and semiprecious stones carved and set in gold and silver—earrings, necklaces, armlets, bracelets, finger rings, jeweled belts and jeweled clasps on their cloaks.

Their paintings show us that they were a people of the sea. Besides the flowers, plants, and elegant court ladies and gentlemen, the artists painted all kinds of sea creatures. Dolphins and flying fish leap in the painted waves of the frescoes around the walls of a royal chamber.

Painted fish swim around the inner sides of a bathtub. Starfish, seaweed, sea shells and the staring eyes and curling arms of the octopus decorate vases, drinking cups and bowls.

It is very odd that the Cretan artists did not leave us any good paintings of their ships. Perhaps they took ships for granted, or considered them merely useful and not beautiful. We have to imagine the long, low, narrow galleys with the oarsmen sitting in rows on their benches along both sides in the hold, singing and pulling their long oars in time to the song. There would be one or perhaps two steersmen in the stern, handling the two steering oars. There would be a mast with the triangle-shaped sail in what is called the lateen rig, like the rigs of ships that sail the Mediterranean coasts today. There would be a cabin or shelter of some sort for the merchant-captain, probably with an awning rigged up to shield him from the sun. The sailors would, of course, have skin browned by the sun, but in the Cretan paintings all the men, even the courtiers, are shown with dark skin of rather reddish tint. The women are painted with a milky white skin, and probably they were careful to keep covered from the burning sun.

Every inch of space in a Cretan ship must have been crammed with boxes and bales and bags of cargo. A Cretan merchant sold lengths of cloth, painted bowls, bronze daggers and knives, strings of beads and all kinds of jewelry. His cargo depended on what the people at the ports on his route would take in exchange for what he wanted to buy.

The Palace of King Minos _____

The palace at Knossos, grandest of all the palaces of
Crete, belonged to King Minos. Minos may have been the
name of the kings at Knossos, or it may have been a title,
in the same way that Pharaoh became the title of the
kings of Egypt. The ruler by this name, or title, apparently
held the power in Crete, and the princes in the other
cities were subject to him. There were palaces built at
several other cities around Crete that followed the same
plan as the palace of King Minos. All these cities had
their harbor towns below on the shore. A very beautiful
palace stands in ruins above the city called Phaistos, on
the southern shore overlooking the Mediterranean. The
snowy peak of Mount Ida, highest of the Cretan mountains, rises behind it. Another palace stood at the eastern
end of the island above Gournia. When Gournia was
excavated, it was found to be a little city of narrow streets
and flat-topped two- and three-story houses. It was full of
craftsmen's workshops and must have been a busy manufacturing town.

King Minos' palace at Knossos looks northward over
the town that was once a port city on the north shore of
Crete. The road from the town climbs to the main gate,
which opens into a large paved court. The court was the
center of the building, and around it the palace rose to
three or more stories. There were pillared arcades around
the court on the ground floor and balconies extending
gracefully above.

The palace was a whole city in itself. It had workshops,

storerooms, offices, a throne room where the king received his ministers and the ambassadors from abroad, a chapel where the priests celebrated the religious rites. Somewhat separated from the rest were the royal apartments, two suites of rooms one above the other for the king and his queen. A private stairway connected them, and each had its own elegant bathroom.

A broad stairway led from the court to the many rooms in the upper stories, and a drainage system of concealed pipes carried the wastes from the bathrooms and toilets as in a modern apartment house. The rooms that did not have windows on the court or the outside walls received their light and air from small courts or light wells, so that even the inner rooms on the ground floor were light and airy.

There were no temples in the Cretan cities. The place of worship was part of the palace and the sacred statues and objects were kept there. The Cretans worshiped a mother goddess, and several beautiful statuettes of her have been found. She is shown wearing the same costume as the court ladies—a long flounced skirt with her tiny waist enclosed in a stiff bodice, and her bosom bare. Her hair falls in a long tress over one shoulder. She wears a crown with a figure of a leopard on it. Some statuettes show her holding a wriggling snake (also a sacred symbol) in each of her outstretched hands.

The bull was another object of worship, and the ceremonies of bull worship were the dramatic part of the Cretan religion. Once a year, for the festival of the bulls, daring hunters went out to capture the great beasts alive and unharmed. Pictures painted on vases and engraved on silver bowls show the hunters luring the bull with a tame cow, and then one of them leaping on his back and grasping his wide-spreading horns.

On the day of the festival the bulls were brought into the palace courtyard for the dances. Slender, graceful boys and girls were trained to perform these dances with the bulls. They danced back and forth and around the animals, ducked under the horns when the beast charged them and rolled nimbly away from his hoofs. The most exciting moment came when one of the youths did not dart away but stood waiting for the bull to charge, and then grasped its horns and turned a somersault over its back. A partner, usually a girl, waited behind to catch him as he vaulted off the bull's back.

This was a dangerous art, probably more dangerous than Spanish bullfighting, and it did not end with the death of the bull. The bulls were herded away after the dances, and only the finest bull was later sacrificed in honor of the god that was most important to a seafaring people, the god of the sea. The Greeks later called this god Poseidon.

The Legend of the Minotaur _____

A thousand years after the Cretans flourished, the Greeks of Athens were telling the story of their young prince of long ago, Prince Theseus, and how he outwitted the great King Minos in his palace with the help of the king's daughter Ariadne. At that time, according to the Greek legend, the people of Athens were subjects of the powerful king of Crete, and they had to pay him a dreadful tribute. Every ninth year they had to choose seven youths and seven maidens who would be taken by ship to Crete and sacrificed to the sacred monster, half bull and half man, that was called the Minotaur, the Minos-bull.

The Minotaur, the story says, was kept in a cave at the end of a long, winding maze of passages called the Labyrinth. Once shut into the Labyrinth, the youth or maiden chosen for the sacrifice would never find the way out, but would wander around and around in the maze, eventually encountering the Minotaur that was waiting to devour its victim.

One year Theseus insisted on going as one of the victims. He was brave and handsome, and when his turn came to go into the Labyrinth the Princess Ariadne took pity on him and gave him a sword and a spool of thread. Theseus killed the Minotaur, found his way out of the Labyrinth by following the thread, set fire to King Minos' palace, and escaped, taking Ariadne and the Athenian youths and maidens with him.

The story of Theseus and the Minotaur was considered only a legend, one of the many marvelous tales of heroes that the Greeks left us in their literature. But early in this century, the English archeologist Sir Arthur Evans discovered the ruins of the great palace at Knossos, and what he found there seemed to confirm a good deal of the Greek tale.

The legend mixed things up, as legends do. There was

no cave of the Minotaur at the palace, only the sacred cave in the mountains. But the description of the Labyrinth might well be a description of the palace itself, where a stranger might become hopelessly lost amid the many stairways, workshops, storerooms, apartments and passages winding around and around the great court and the smaller courts. The monster, half bull and half man, was an imaginary part of the legend. But bulls were there, pictured everywhere on the walls, the vases and the beautiful bowls and goblets that were found. Horns of bulls adorned the shrines, along with the *labys*, the sacred double ax, for which the Labyrinth was named. And there were the pictures of the young bull dancers, boys and girls, somersaulting over the backs of the charging bulls. Most interesting of all, the palace had indeed been destroyed by fire.

So although some part of the legend is surely storyteller's fancy, some part is history. King Minos was a rich and powerful ruler, and no doubt he did demand tribute from the towns and smaller cities that he conquered with his strong navy. It is also likely that part of the tribute was taken in the form of young captives who could be trained for the bull dances. But did Theseus burn down the palace? The ruins show that the palace was burned and destroyed several times, probably by earthquakes and the fires that resulted when lighted lamps were overturned and ovens were shattered. Each time the palace was rebuilt, and each time it was grander than before.

The last time was different. The disaster came suddenly.

The artisans and artists were at their work in the palace workshops when it happened, and their tools and half-finished work have been found in the shops under layers of ashes. All the evidence showed that there had been a terrible fire. But there was one strange point. All the most valuable objects, the metal vessels and decorations, were missing, as though the place had been looted before it was burned. So it is possible that the great palace was finally destroyed by invaders from the sea. The next palace that was built on the site was much smaller and more modest, and this may be a sign that the greatness of Crete had finally come to an end.

In Athens the story of Theseus at the palace of King Minos was considered not a tale but a part of history. For hundreds of years the Athenians preserved the ship in which he and his companions were said to have come safely home. They kept it in repair and used it for important state voyages.

The Raiders

It is hard to believe that Theseus and a handful of Greek boys and girls could have looted and burned the palace of the sea king and ended his great power. But from excavations not only on Crete itself but in Greece and on other shores of the eastern Mediterranean and its arm, the Aegean Sea, archeologists have pieced together a more believable account of what may have happened.

When the cities of Crete began to develop their control over the eastern sea, they founded colonies of their own people on the mainland coasts of Greece and the nearby islands. At about the same time a new people began coming into Greece, an Indo-European people from the Asian steppes who called themselves Achaeans.

Gradually these early Greek immigrants spread through the peninsula of Greece and the islands, displacing the Cretans or, more likely, intermarrying with them. They were a wandering people of horsemen and herdsmen, and their gods were sky gods instead of gods and goddesses of the earth and fertility. On the rocky Greek soil they could not do very much farming, but they grew olives, grapes and a little grain and they pastured their herds and horses on the rugged hillsides. And they became seafarers. At first their young men learned sailing in the Cretan merchant ships. Later on they began to build their own ships and sail out to do business for themselves. But they still had to pay taxes or tribute to the Cretan king who ruled the eastern seas.

By the time that Theseus is supposed to have gone to Crete, the Greeks had built their own towns and were ruled by their own princes. One town that was becoming quite rich and powerful was Mycenae. It stood on the southern peninsula of Greece, which is nearly cut off by water except for a narrow strip of land, later called the Isthmus of Corinth. (Ships sail right across it now, through the Corinth Canal.) Another small kingdom north of this isthmus on the eastern shore was Attica, and its capital was Athens. Athens was built on a rocky height overlooking the sea, and its king, Aegeus, was Theseus' father. Aegeus' name was later given to the Aegean Sea, that part of the Mediterranean north of Crete in which the Greek islands extend along the shores of Greece and Turkey all the way to the Anatolian coast of Asia.

At the same time that the Greeks were building up their own trade in their own ships and sailing from their own towns and harbors, many of their merchants were established in the Cretan cities as well. At the time when Prince Theseus is supposed to have gone to the palace of King Minos, the harbor town of Knossos was already full of Greek-speaking Achaeans. There were Greek businessmen, tradesmen and sailors in all the port cities around the island and numbers of Greek ships in all the harbors.

We cannot know whether Theseus came to the festival as a captive for the bull dancing or as a visiting prince from a subject land. Either way, he could have come as the leader of a plot to win independence from the Cretan overlords, and the celebration of the bull festival would have been the perfect opportunity. At such a time, when the Cretans were feasting and drinking on their great holiday of the year, the Greeks in Knossos and all the port cities could have risen in the night with swords and torches, setting fires, looting the palaces and rich houses, killing and taking Cretan captives, capturing or sinking the Cretan ships in the harbors.

This may be the history behind both the legend of Theseus and the terrible fire that destroyed King Minos' splendid palace. From then on, the power of Crete declined. Many Cretan merchants and craftsmen fled to the eastern shore of the Mediterranean, where they had trading connections in Byblos, Sidon and other cities along the coast. Hundreds of years later their descendants were probably among the Philistines whom the Israelites fought for Palestine and the Phoenicians with whom King Solomon made his profitable alliance.

Meanwhile the Greeks grew in strength and power until they made the Aegean their own sea.

Part 7

People of a Heroic Age

The Achaeans were the heroes of Greece. Twenty-five hundred years ago, boys and girls in Athens grew up knowing the stories of the great deeds and adventures of Achilles the great warrior, clever Odysseus, King Agamemnon and his brother Menelaus, wise old Nestor, and their conquest of Troy, in the same way that children today know about King Arthur and his Knights of the Round Table, or about Davy Crockett and Daniel Boone.

The Achaeans were Indo-Europeans, and they were part of the general movement of tribesmen into the settled lands. Some of the Indo-European tribes had taken over the mountainous land of Iran, between Mesopotamia and India. One great body of them, the Aryans, had swept through the Indus River cities and were taking over most of India.

The Achaeans may have come south through Anatolia. They may have come to Greece and the islands originally as colonists from Troy. Or they may have come by a more westward route, through the Balkan lands of eastern Europe and down into Greece. Wandering peoples do not build on the land, and without such traces, we cannot be sure what routes they followed. Once they settle, however, they leave their marks.

The wandering Indo-European tribes did leave marks of another kind, however: a form of language different from the language of the original dwellers in the place, and different also from the languages of the Semitic tribes coming from the south. Scholars trace these language differences in the names of places and the names of kings

127

and warriors that are mentioned in the records of established nations that had a written language, like Egypt or Babylon. And so, although the Indo-European tribes had no written language when they came into the settled lands, we read the names of their nations and their kings, and the towns and cities they built for themselves, in the business accounts of the merchants who traded with them, the letters of a Pharaoh to his governors of subject lands and theirs to him, or the inscription on a monument boasting of the conquests of a warrior king.

The wanderers from the steppes of western Asia and eastern Europe were a horse-breeding people, and their thrust into the settled world came in the form of warriors in swift chariots. This new kind of fighting threw old-fashioned armies and even fortified cities into panic because they knew how fast an army on foot could travel but not the speed of an army on wheels. Even a small force could conquer by a surprise attack, as we have seen in the ruins of Mohenjo-Daro. Soon all the nations, even the Egyptians, were adding chariot regiments to their armies (and kings and noblemen were going hunting and traveling in the new vehicles). Later the Indo-European invaders learned to ride, and they came as cavalry, much swifter and very much more dangerous. Some scholars believe that the legends of the Centaurs, half man and half horse, grew out of people's first terrifying sight of men on horseback.

But the Indo-Europeans were not only warriors and destructive raiders. The horse-breeders from the north brought a new vigor and imagination to the settled world of established empires and rich, sophisticated cities.

The First Greeks _____

Like their fellow Indo-Europeans who had come south before them, the Achaeans were an energetic people. They came into the Aegean lands about four thousand years ago, and they were probably the first Greek-speaking people in the settled world. They seem to have taken over the colonies established by Crete on the Greek mainland, and at first they were subject to Crete. Whether or not they brought about the fall of Crete, they took advantage of it.

The peninsula into which they came was wild country, rocky and mountainous. Deer, bears, wolves and fierce wild boars roamed the forests. Wild grapes and olives grew there, and there was plenty of pasture for their cattle and horses but not much level land for plowing.

On the other hand, Greece was surrounded on three sides by the sea and its shores were deeply indented with coves and bays which made excellent sheltered harbors. The sea was sprinkled with islands, so that a ship could sail all the way south to Crete or east to Asia without ever losing sight of land. Sailors could beach their boats and wait out a storm. They could pull ashore every evening before dark, roast a good supper of fish or freshly caught game, sleep safely on land at night and fill their animal-skin bottles with fresh water from a spring before embarking again the next morning.

The Achaeans did a little farming, all that was necessary to feed their families. They bred and tended their horses, cattle and pigs. They hunted, both for food and for pleasure. And they went to sea to make their fortune.

These early Greeks cared little for learning and did not bother to learn reading and writing, even though by that time many countries around the Mediterranean had written languages and professional scribes. The Achaeans were vigorous outdoor men who delighted in hard games like foot races and contests in throwing the spear and the javelin. They ate great hearty meals of a bullock or a pig roasted whole over an open fire. The Greeks in their legends called the Achaean leaders kings, but from the evidences of their way of life they were rather clan chieftains who worked side by side with their retainers, chopping and sawing wood, building their own houses and furniture. Their houses were not palaces like those of Crete, but citadels of stone and timber, with a central fireplace in the main room and not much furniture. The women spun and wove the wool from their sheep and goats, and made blankets and clothing. Fleeces and animal pelts were used for rugs, bed coverings and cloaks in the chilly Greek climate. As the archeologists and historians reconstruct it, it was a way of life much like the life of the early Middle Ages in Europe.

The Achaeans had noble rules of hospitality. In a wild land, where travel was hard and dangerous, a traveler who could give a good account of himself found food and shelter in their houses for as long as he cared to stay. They gave him fresh clothes if his own were worn or soiled, and gifts to take with him when he left. And although they neither read nor wrote, they loved a good rousing story of adventure. They had minstrels, harpers and poets to entertain them around the fire. A traveler was expected to entertain his host and hostess after supper with the story of his travels, sitting by the fire and drinking wine mixed with water.

The Achaeans admired fighting skill and loved a battle. Their weapons were short heavy swords, battle axes, spears and daggers. They wore leather body armor, leather and metal helmets studded with boar tusks, and they carried body-sized leather shields.

When they took to the sea, they learned to be excellent sailors. But they did not, at first, become honest businessmen. They became pirates and sea raiders, prowling along the coast for slow, heavily laden cargo ships to plunder and rich towns to raid and loot. While the sea kings of Crete were still in power, the shipping lanes were kept safe for merchant ships. But after Crete fell and its navy no longer patrolled the waters, the shipping and the harbor towns were fair game for sea raiders.

The Achaeans were not the only sea raiders of the time. Daring sailors from all around the Mediterranean, from European and North African coast towns, were darting along the eastern Mediterranean shores, plundering the ships and the towns. Even powerful Egypt was suffering from the raids of the People of the Sea, as they were called. Some of the raiders were looking for new homes, plun-

dering along the way, carrying their families and all their
belongings with them in their swift boats. During this
time a number of peoples who had come from the north
to the Mediterranean shores, as the Achaeans had done,
were establishing themselves in Italy, Sicily, Sardinia and
northern Africa west of Egypt.

A blind poet, Homer, is believed to be the author of two
long story poems about the Achaeans. The *Iliad* tells of
the siege of Troy (or Ilion, the Greek name for the same
city). With Agamemnon, king of Mycenae, as their leader,
the Greek heroes set out in a thousand ships to win back
Helen, the beautiful queen of Sparta and wife of Menelaus. While Menelaus was absent, she had been stolen
away by Paris, the handsome young prince of Troy.

The poem tells how the Greeks besieged Troy for ten
years, and during that time Achilles, young Paris, his elder
brother Hector, who was the great hero of the Trojans,
and many others were killed. Then Odysseus had the
idea of building a huge wooden horse and hiding with
some companions inside it while the Greeks boarded their
ships and sailed away as though they had given up the
war. The Trojans, unsuspecting, took the horse into the
city, and in the night Odysseus and his comrades stole
out and opened the city gates. The Greeks meanwhile had
returned, and they stormed into the city, killing and looting, and finally burned it to the ground.

Other Greek legends complete the story. Menelaus took
his beautiful wife back to Sparta and from that time on
she was known as Helen of Troy. Agamemnon sailed
safely home, only to be killed by his wife and a cousin

who had taken over the kingdom during his long absence. Odysseus was shipwrecked and spent ten years in dangerous adventures all over the Mediterranean before he came home to his wife Penelope in his palace in Ithaca. Homer's second great poem, the *Odyssey*, tells the story of Odysseus' wanderings, his encounters with the one-eyed giant, Cyclops, the Sirens whose enticing singing caused sailors to wreck their ships on the rocks, and the sorceress Circe, who turned Odysseus' men into swine because they made such greedy pigs of themselves at her supper table.

For hundreds of years Homer's story of the siege of Troy was thought to be a legend. It was read in the same way that the story of Theseus at the palace of King Minos was read, as a marvelous invention of the poet's imagination, or else a collection of tales that the old storytellers had made up to entertain the people and that Homer had put together in one long poem.

But then archeologists discovered the burned city of Troy, just as they later discovered the burned palace at Knossos in Crete. And they discovered the great stone citadel of Mycenae, the place where the poem said Agamemnon had his palace. They found graves there containing the same kinds of weapons, helmets and armor, the gold and silver cups and other objects that Homer had described. They found traces of the palace with the great hall, the raised fireplace in the center, the tall wooden pillars holding up the high roof, the pillared porch where the slaves and sometimes the guests slept in Homer's tale.

The Homes of the Heroes _____

From the excavations at Mycenae, and from palaces and graves at other places in Greece where Homer's heroes were said to have lived, archeologists have put together a picture of the way of life of the early Greeks, the people of a heroic age, and also what were probably the historical facts of the war with Troy. What they found at Mycenae was especially interesting. It was grand enough to be the stronghold of Agamemnon as he appeared in Homer's story, the most powerful king in Greece and the commander of the entire Greek army that embarked against Troy.

The ruins at Mycenae stand out against the sky on a rocky height, above what must have been a cluster of farms and villages on the plain. The fortress walls are of double thickness, built of huge slabs of stone. The great gateway is still there, with two lions sculptured in stone above it. Only the muscular bodies of the lions remain. Their heads, which may have been carved out of some more valuable stone like marble or alabaster, disappeared long ago.

Within a ring of the massive stone wall are a number of tombs, and these are also massive. One group of graves was dug into the earth in the form of shafts. Another and probably later type of tomb was in the form of a domed chamber, like a gigantic beehive, built out of enormous blocks of stone. The stone blocks were so well fitted that the lofty dome is still standing without a crack or a loose stone. A stone stairway leading down into one of the tombs is lined along its sides with the same kind of great stone slabs, and the entrance and the steps are built of massive blocks of stone.

When the archeologists found the graves, most had already been robbed of the treasure that had been placed there with the bodies of the dead kings and queens. But some gold ornaments still remained. One of these was a mask, made out of a thin sheet of gold and shaped to fit over the face of a dead king. At first it was believed that the grave in which it was found was Agamemnon's and that the mask was his portrait, but more careful dating showed that it was made before the time of the Trojan war.

Finding the city of Troy was a sensational discovery. Under the mound the archeologists found not one but nine settlements, some more like towns or villages than cities, all built one above the other on the same site. The seventh Troy, just below the two top levels of buildings, was the Troy of the Greek siege, of about thirty-two hundred years ago. Far below it, in the second Troy, a much older city, a great treasure of gold and jewelry was found, so it was clear that Troy was indeed a rich city, and had been so for a long time, long before the Greeks were strong enough to compete with it.

The Story Behind the Story

And so we now treat Homer's story of the Trojan War as history, just as the Greeks always did, but it is history told as a tale of high adventure, with considerable poetic embroidery, as the Theseus story is embellished. The siege of Troy took place five or six hundred years before Homer sang about it and about two hundred years after the destruction of Minos' palace and the end of the power of Crete, which Achaeans like those who destroyed Troy may also have brought about.

The Achaeans may have made war on Troy because of the runaway Helen. No one can say whether the beautiful queen of Sparta ever actually existed. But they also had a strong commercial rivalry with Troy, and if Helen really did elope with Paris, she may have provided them with a good excuse to attack their rival.

After the fall of Crete the Achaeans were in the strategic position to take over control of the eastern waters and the Mediterranean trade. They were the strongest people, after the Cretans, on the Aegean Sea. They had made their homes and built their fortified palaces on most of the Greek mainland and on many of the two hundred twenty islands that lie in the Aegean between Greece and Crete to the south and between Greece and the Anatolian coast of Asia to the east.

Troy was a tiny city, not much more than a walled town in size, but it was a busy trading center, and was wealthy and strongly fortified. It stood on a rocky headland right at the mouth of the narrow strait that separates Asia from Europe, which we call the Dardanelles and the Greeks called the Hellespont.

The Hellespont is the gateway to the water route from

the Mediterranean to the Black Sea, and all around the Black Sea were plains where quantities of grain were produced. The Hellespont was also the connecting link between the Mediterranean trade and the mountain people of western Asia and eastern Europe, who mined metals and had many other valuable products to trade. Troy sat at the crossroads of land and sea routes and grew rich on the shipping and caravan trade of a whole corner of the ancient world.

The Achaean Greeks of the mainland and the islands had strong links with the Anatolian coast of Asia south of Troy. There was an Achaean kingdom called Lydia on that coast. In Homer's story the Greeks had close links even with the Trojans against whom they were making war, and that was not surprising. They were all descended from the same wandering tribes, the Indo-Europeans from the steppes north of the Black and Caspian seas.

The mountainous peninsula of Anatolia reaches out from Asia to form the northern arm of the Mediterranean crescent. It was not only a bridge from Asia to Europe. It was also a bridge from the wild lands of the north to the rich cities and the great empires of Egypt and Mesopotamia, and the crowded lands between.

The Indo-European tribes had been coming south across that bridge for centuries. On the high plateau of central Anatolia, one of the tribal peoples had established a powerful military kingdom, the kingdom of the Hittites. Another group, the Hurrians, had moved farther south. Still another, the Mitanni, had become the aristocratic rulers over the farm population of one region, and they hired themselves out as mercenary soldiers to other ambitious rulers.

After their conquest of Troy, the Achaeans were not given time to regain their strength and resources in order to enjoy the fruits of their victory. A new wave of Greek-speaking people, the Dorians, were coming down from the north into Greece, and for some hundreds of years Greece was torn with the wars of competing kings and chieftains. Eventually the newcomers overran most of Greece, capturing even the powerful citadel of Mycenae and sailing across to take over much of Crete. Many of the original Greek settlers fled to the islands and the Asian coast of the Aegean and settled in the towns of their Greek-speaking relatives or established new towns of their own.

In their own history the Greeks gave the name of Ionia to this coast and the islands, and the people of Ionia claimed that Attica was their original homeland and Athens was their mother city. In fact their language was the Attic or Athenian dialect, different from the Greek of the Dorians, so that there is some basis in history for their claim.

The Dorians finally established their stronghold in the military city-state of Sparta, the legendary home of Menelaus and Helen. The Spartans cared as little for literature and learning as had the Achaeans who conquered Troy. In the next centuries it was the cities of Ionia, along the Asian coast, that gave rise to the philosophy, science, poetry and art which came to their height in the golden age of Athens.

Part 8

People of the Frontier

In the world of five thousand years ago the continent of Europe was an unexplored wilderness. If the farmers and city builders in the eastern lands knew of Europe at all, they probably thought of it in the way the first settlers in Massachusetts or Virginia thought of the American West, as a wild country full of dangerous beasts and savage men. We know that some of these New England and Virginia people began to feel crowded, and they did venture westward little by little, looking for new farmland. It was the same in the ancient world. Farmers from the eastern Mediterranean had already begun to move into the wilds of Europe.

The merchants and traders were moving in too. They were looking for metals in the wilderness lands. Their galleys nosed along the Mediterranean shores, finding routes into the wild continent.

One such trading route began about where Venice now stands, at the mouth of the river Po. It followed the river up into the Alps, to a mountain pass called the Camonica Valley, and there the merchants from the east met tribesmen from the north. The tribesmen brought furs to trade as well as something much more valuable, the "sea gold," amber, that they gathered on the beaches of the northern seas after a storm. Amber is the fossilized resin of ancient trees that were drowned when Ice Age glaciers melted and the seas rose.

Another trade route began at the border between

France and Spain, where the Pyrenees mountains come down to the Mediterranean shore. The route went up along the Loire River valley into France and perhaps north to the English Channel coast. Still another route went by sea around the Spanish peninsula and up the Atlantic coast of Europe, to southern Ireland, England and perhaps as far as Scandinavia on the North Sea.

The Wilderness Peoples

What kind of people did the merchants meet in the western wilderness? They were people of different kinds, making their living in different ways. Some were still living like the Ice Age cavemen who hunted the hairy mammoths, the woolly rhinoceros and the reindeer.

When the ice melted away from northern Europe toward the Arctic and forests began to cover the land, the mammoths and the other big game disappeared. But the reindeer followed the ice northward, and some of the Ice Age hunters followed them. The hunters lived very much as the Laplanders still live in the far north of Europe on the Arctic tundra, following the reindeer herds. They hunted these animals not only for the meat but for bones and antlers to use for weapons and hides for clothing, tents and skin boats.

Some of the people who stayed behind never learned to make use of the forests, to chop down trees and work with the wood. They lived poorly, huddled in small family groups on the edges of the forest. Their stone tools were small, and were useful only for hunting small animals like squirrels and rabbits.

Some moved to the seashores and ate the shellfish that they could pick off the sea bottom in shallow water. Along the Danish coasts there are gigantic heaps of oyster shells, mixed with ancient tools made of flint and deer antler, bone harpoons, spears, nets, fishhooks and broken bits of pottery. The people there had turned their backs on the forest and learned to live quite well from the sea. They had learned to make clay pots for cooking nourishing soups and stews out of otherwise useless scraps. Everything we know about these people we have learned from their garbage dumps, or middens, and so they are called the Kitchen Midden People.

How they learned to make real pottery, baked hard in the fire, we can only guess. In Egypt and Mesopotamia the first potters had the hot sun to bake their clay pots before they learned to build ovens, or kilns. But on the wet and foggy shores of the Baltic and the North Sea the sun rarely shines and it is never very hot. Possibly the women had taken to making clay containers in which to store seeds or nuts they had gathered, to keep the squirrels from getting them. And possibly a clay jar had accidentally fallen into the fire and hardened enough to hold liquids without leaking; the people would have discovered that it could be set over the fire without burning. Their pots were lumpy mud-colored vessels, with pointed bottoms that could be pushed firmly into an earth floor or wedged between stones over the fire. The people did not try to decorate or beautify them. But they were a fine invention for the time.

Some of the wilderness people, the ones who lived in northern Europe and Britain about ten to five thousand years ago, learned to live with the forest. The climate was steadily growing warmer and wetter, and they matched their way of life to the changing environment.

The ice was melting away to the north, the seas were rising, Britain and Ireland were no longer attached to the continent and the northern coast had been carved into the Scandinavian peninsula and the islands and peninsula of Denmark. Little by little the forest trees grew northward. First came the birches and willows that could live in the cold, and after them, the pines. These were slender trees that made thin forests in which a hunter could see the deer and hunt them with bow and arrow.

As the land grew warmer and wetter, oak forests replaced them, and brought a thick underbrush of hazel, alder and all kinds of woodland shrubs. The deer still browsed there, and wild pigs, foxes, beaver, wolves lived in them. Fish were also plentiful in the lakes and seas as well as whales and seals.

The people settled mostly around lakes and lowland ponds. What we know of them has been discovered by digging in the swamps and peat bogs that were once those ancient lakes, and so they are called the Great Bog People. Their first invention for living in the forest was an ax that could chop down trees, and after that they learned the many uses of wood. They began with nothing more than half a deer antler, with the long shaft for a handle and one sharpened prong to chop with. Then they fixed a flint ax blade to the antler handle, and later on they made a holder for the flint out of antler bone and a wooden handle to fit into the holder.

They went on to invent a whole kit of carpenters' tools out of stone, antler bone and wood. They made boats for fishing and traveling, and sledges on runners to haul their game back to camp or to carry their possessions to a new camping site. They tamed the dog, probably by throwing scraps to the smallest of the wolves that skulked around the camp. With the domestication of the dog they gained a valuable hunting companion that could track and even bring down a deer in the forest.

The Bog People never settled in villages, but remained wandering hunters and fishermen. They had plenty of space because in all of Europe at that time there were no more than perhaps a million people altogether, scattered about in small bands that never met each other from one year to the next. The Bog People stayed in the lowlands and the swampy forests. But up in the mountains of Switzerland there were people who also lived at the edges of the lakes, and they built villages.

The Lake Dwellers of Switzerland were farmers who also fished and hunted small game. They chose lake shores where there was some space between the edge of the forest and the water, and so they did not have the hard work of clearing the land. They built their villages on this soft boggy ground by driving the trunks of small trees into the earth in upright rows, and then laying a floor of branches, rubble and earth on crossbeams set between the piles. Or they made the floor first, and drove the piles down through it to anchor it in the soft ground.

All these peoples in Europe were living a primitive wilderness life at the same time that city life was developing in the eastern lands. Except for the Swiss Lake Dwellers, who built villages, grew crops and kept domestic animals for food, not just dogs for hunting, all of them were still living the life that men had lived for a million years, wandering, hunting, fishing and food-gathering. They were the last people of that vanishing way of life, halfway between the hunters and the farmers, and now the farmers were beginning to take over the land.

The Immigrants⎯⎯⎯⎯⎯⎯⎯⎯⎯⎯⎯

Farmers from the Mediterranean were moving up the Danube River valley, and farmers were coming into other river valleys. Farmers were growing crops on the southern downs of England.

They were all still using stone tools. In some parts of northern Europe and in England and Ireland there were what we might call factories for stone tools. These were places where the hillsides were strewn with boulders or where cliffs thrust out of the earth, with the kinds of stone that made good axes, hatchets or knives. Some of the hunting tribes had become particularly skillful at stoneworking, and every year they came down from their hunting grounds to spend a season at these places, making a supply of stone tools. Then they would take their new stock to the farmers' market in the lowlands, to trade for the grain and barley out of which they would make their bread and beer for the rest of the year.

The first farmers in Europe settled on land where the forest had not taken over, like the Swiss Lake Dwellers and the villagers on the English downs. Where they had to clear the forest for planting, their method was to chop down the trees and then burn off the stumps and underbrush.

Two Danish archeologists decided to see how clearing with such primitive stone tools was done. They borrowed flint ax blades from the Copenhagen museum, set them into wooden handles like those of the ancient farmers, and found that once they learned how to use the axes, they could chop down an oak tree a foot thick in half an hour. They cleared two acres of all the trees, left one acre simply cleared and burned off the other with brush fires, a job that took between three and four days. Then they planted seeds of the early kinds of wheat and barley that the first farmers had grown. On the acre that they had not burned, very little grew. The forest soil was too acid to grow crops. But the burned-over acre grew a fine crop. The archeologists completed this interesting experiment by harvesting the crop as the ancient farmers had, with a flint sickle and a flint knife.

By this method, called slash-and-burn, the first farmers

in Europe cleared a piece of land, farmed it until the crops became too poor in the exhausted soil, then moved on and cut out another clearing. Meanwhile their farm animals grazed over the old cleared land and kept the forest from growing up again.

In Europe five thousand years ago there was a whole continent of forests, plains and fertile valleys, still uncrowded or even uninhabited, but since then most of the forest land of Europe has been converted to farm and pasture land. When there was no more free land to move to, farmers learned to restore the soil by more careful cultivation and by spreading the manure of the farm animals to fertilize the fields.

New People, New Ways

Farmer colonists began moving into eastern Europe as far back as eight thousand years ago. On the plain of Macedonia in northern Greece, near the modern village of Nea Nikomedia, a settlement was found that dates from that time. The people had learned to cut the hard forest trees of Europe, and their little one-room houses were made of oak, plastered over with mud to make them snug against cold and wet. They raised crops of lentils, wheat and barley, and they kept sheep, goats, a few cows and some pigs. They hunted a little, and ate fish and shellfish from the sea and from the ancient freshwater lake next to their village. Farmers like these are believed to have come from the nearby Asian and eastern Mediterranean lands. They spread into eastern Europe and all the way to Scandinavia.

Another group of farm immigrants came into western Europe from the Mediterranean, and they are believed to have come from the Greek islands by way of Malta, Sicily, Italy, southern France and eastern Spain, probably also from across the sea in North Africa. They spread northward to the British Isles and eastward into Germany and Switzerland, and the Swiss Lake Dwellers may originally have been part of this group.

As the farmers cleared more and more of the forest lands, the old-fashioned hunting people had to move farther and farther north to find enough game. They moved into the forests of Finland and northern Scandinavia, and there were still hunters in northern England and the Scottish highlands when the farm villages on the southern downs were already old.

All these movements of peoples were slow. The farmers moved only when they had to clear new land, perhaps a mile or two every few years. It took about three thousand years for the new way of life to reach the northern parts of Europe.

The farmers still used stone tools, but they did not merely chip the blades to make an edge, in the old way. They knew how to grind and polish the stone to make it really sharp. They made good clay pots and they spun and wove cloth. In Italy, Spain and southern France they grew olives, and there and farther north they grew grapes.

The Great Stone Builders _____

A strange custom that grew up among these western European farmers along the coast was the building of tombs and holy places with enormous stone slabs. They cut and hauled stones weighing as much as forty tons, sometimes from considerable distances, and then set them up on end on an open field or hilltop, in circles or parallel rows. At Carnac in Brittany, in the northern part of France, there is a field with three thousand such stones in eleven parallel rows, some of them still standing upright on end as they were originally placed. One stone found in Brittany was sixty-five feet tall before it toppled and broke.

Stonehenge, in southern England, is the most famous of these great stone shrines, although it was built at a later time. In another shrine, not far away at Avebury, the circle of stones is so large that a whole modern village is enclosed within it.

The tombs were built with huge stone slabs lined up to form long underground passageways, with stone-built chambers opening off the passageways. The chambers were sometimes round and domed, sometimes rectangular, and each chamber was used for many burials. At New Grange in Ireland, about twenty-five miles from Dublin, there are many such passage graves, and the largest of them has a passage sixty-two feet long. The main chamber of this impressive tomb is nearly twenty feet high. There is a cemetery of graves of this kind on the island of Malta, and another at Los Millares in Spain.

The stones in these monuments are roughly cut and unpolished, but some of them are carved. They have strange symbols on them, in the shape of circles, triangles, spirals, a face made in a series of irregular ovals, a single eye.

The archeologists have named this style of building megalithic, from two Greek words, *megas*, meaning "great," and *lithos*, meaning "stone." The symbols carved on the stones are thought to belong to the worship of a mother goddess, or earth goddess, who was believed to bring fertility to the soil.

No one really knows where this style of building came from, or who the people were who built in this way. One theory is that merchants from the Aegean brought it with them, and taught the people both the religion and the megalithic style of building. The walls and tombs of Mycenae and other citadels of that time in Greece are also built of huge stones, but there are no shrines or tombs exactly like the European ones there or anywhere in the eastern Mediterranean.

Stonehenge is not the oldest nor the largest of the megalithic shrines, but it is the best known and the one most people go to see. It stands alone in the center of the vast, bare Salisbury Plain, a striking sight even from far away. The mystery of the giant stones in their circles hangs like a magic spell over the place, and it becomes stranger and more mysterious the closer one comes to it.

For hundreds of years the people who lived near Stonehenge believed that the great stones had been brought there and placed upright in their circles by giants, or else

by magic. They could not imagine that ordinary men could
have dragged and lifted them into position, and they felt
that there was great and probably dangerous magic about
the place. Of course Stonehenge was not built by giants
nor by magic, but by men. It was first built about four
thousand years ago and was rebuilt several hundred years
later, with more of the giant stones arranged in still more
complicated patterns.

An ancient avenue, built up and banked on both sides,
leads to the first stone, called the Hele Stone, which
stands upright outside the great circle. The circle originally consisted of thirty giant stones standing upright,
with slabs laid across their tops like the lintel of a door-
way, each slab fitted into grooves or slots on the standing
stones. Each of the standing stones is 13½ feet high,
more than twice the height of a tall man, and each one is
dug 4½ feet into the ground. Originally the lintel stones
across the tops were connected to each other all the way
around, making a closed circle.

Within the great circle is an oval of somewhat smaller
stones standing upright, then a horseshoe of giant upright stones in pairs with lintel stones across their tops.
Then there is a double row of small upright stones, and in
the center is a single stone like an altar.

The stones were chipped and hacked to the right size
and shape with stone hammers and mauls, and some of
these tools have been found in the foundation holes,
thrown in to wedge the giant slabs firmly in their place.
Each stone was put into its place according to careful

measurements. The Hele Stone was so placed that at Mid-
summer's Day, the longest day of the year, when the sun
is at its most northerly point, the rising sun casts the
shadow of the Hele Stone exactly on the Altar Stone in the
center of the shrine. Other stones were also placed to
mark the positions of the sun and moon at certain times
of the year. The stones seem to have been set out as a holy
calendar marking the important dates of the year, the
dates when religious festivals must be held to honor the
sun and the moon.

The labor that went into building such a shrine was
something like the labor of building the pyramids in Egypt.
Some of the giant stones came from Wales, and they were
brought part of the way by sea, but they still had to be
loaded and unloaded, and hauled to their place on sledges,
probably by the entire population of able-bodied men
pulling ropes of cowhide or woven out of cow hair. Then
each slab had to be levered off its sledge and into the hole
prepared for it, and then slowly raised on end by men
lifting it an inch or two at a time with levers while other
men pushed logs under to hold it up. Each lintel stone had
to be lifted inch by inch in the same way, on logs gradually
piled up to a framework more than thirteen feet high.
Then men standing on the top had to lever it onto the
standing stones and into the grooves that had been
chipped out for it.

A small carving of Greek axes and a dagger was
found not long ago on one of the stones. No one can
say for certain whether these were put there by Greek

architects and workmen who had come to help with the
building, but no better explanation of the carvings has
been suggested.

Whether or not the early Greeks taught the early
Europeans to build their great stone monuments, there
were amber ornaments in the tombs of Mycenae and the
amber could only have come from northern Europe, so
there was certainly trading going on between these peoples.

No one knows when the amber trade with the northmen
of Europe began, but the route through the Alpine passes
is very old. On the faces of the rocks in the Camonica
Valley there is a whole history carved out, in thousands of
pictures, telling how the valley people learned new ways
from the travelers and traders over a period of several
thousand years.

The oldest pictures were religious, showing odd little
human figures with their arms raised in prayer, and a
round disk for the sun, which these Alpine people worshiped. In some pictures the sun disk is held up by a tall
figure of a man, while around him others seem to be
dancing, wearing hairy masks and costumes which may
have been animal skins, and carrying swords and axes in
their hands. Later the sun is shown riding in a chariot,
telling us that the taming of horses and the making of
chariots had come to this European mountain center, perhaps from the Indo-Europeans of the steppes who were
coming into Europe, or from the merchants of Mycenae
and the Aegean islands.

The rock pictures show animals, and the nets, traps
and stone weapons of a hunting people. They show the

simple plows of the first farmers, the little peak-roofed houses they lived in, the looms on which they wove the fleece of their sheep into cloth. About thirty-six hundred years ago they learned how to use the copper in their mountains to make metal tools, vessels and weapons. The pictures of about that time show chariots and bronze daggers like those of Mycenae, and a bronze blade made in the Camonica Valley has actually been found in a grave in Mycenae.

More Newcomers

New people and new ways still came into Europe. Some time after the megalith builders, a people called the Beaker Folk came northward through western Europe and into England. Their odd name comes from the fact that all we know of them we learned from what they buried with their dead. They always placed a peculiar kind of bell-shaped beaker, or drinking cup, made of clay and gracefully decorated, in their graves. They also placed with the body an oblong curved plaque made of stone or bone and with a hole at each corner. This turned out to be the arm guard that an archer fastens above his wrist on the inner side of the arm that holds the bow, to protect his arm from being scraped by the bowstring.

These objects are evidence that the Beaker Folk were skilled in pottery and archery. They had a third skill more important than either of these. They were metalworkers. The evidence suggests that they came from Spain, where

the Aegean merchants went to buy copper and tin that
was mined out of the hills. These merchants brought back
to sell to the miners the bronze daggers, tools and beautiful objects made from that same copper and tin by the
metalworkers of the eastern Mediterranean. Apparently
the miners in Spain decided that they too could use their
copper and tin to make bronze and to forge fine weapons
and tools. Once they had learned the art, they began to
trade on their own.

They traveled north first as merchants, to sell their
bronze wares to the farmers who were still using stone
tools. Then they established colonies, bringing their metal-
working forges with them and using the copper and tin
from the hills of the north. And so at last the use of
stone for tools and weapons disappeared, as the hunting
life had disappeared. Stone gave way to bronze, but only
for a while, because bronze was already giving way to
iron, which some of the Indo-European peoples had by
that time brought to the eastern lands.

In eastern Europe the same change was taking place.
It is not certain whether the mountain people in the Bal-
kans, who first began to work with metal, learned their art
from the Mediterranean and Asian merchants or developed it for themselves.

The next group to enter Europe after the Beaker Folk
were the Battle Ax People, and their name is taken from
the polished stone battle axes that were all they left behind them when they vanished. These were beautiful objects, sometimes for use as weapons, sometimes so large
and heavy that they could only be for ceremonial use or

as symbols of office, like a king's scepter. They were made of fine stone that could be polished until it shone.

The Battle Ax People traveled across Europe all the way to the Atlantic. They had come from the steppes of Russia somewhere near the Black Sea, and they were another of the wandering Indo-European peoples. Like all these tribes they were herdsmen, with cattle that gave them meat, milk and hides, and they had tamed the wild horses of the steppes and rode behind them in fast light chariots. They took land for their pastures and they taught the European farmers how to use horses. Probably they gave up their wandering life, settled down to farming and mingled with the local inhabitants, because nothing more is known about them. But they brought with them the language from which all the European languages are derived.

The Battle Ax People may not have been the first Indo-Europeans to come into northern Europe, only the first of whom some slight traces have been found. But after them new waves of herdsmen, charioteers and finally horsemen moved across Europe from the eastern steppes, bringing their arts and their Indo-European languages to the west.

About four thousand years ago, a blend of all these European peoples appeared, who called themselves the Celts. They had a common language and they knew the metalworking arts. In the next centuries they spread across the heart of Europe westward into France, England and Ireland. Theirs was a princely style of life, their handicrafts were exquisite, and almost the only art they did not possess was the art of writing. Julius Caesar gained his great fame by conquering them in France, where the Romans called them the Gauls. They followed a dark forest religion, and their priests, called the Druids, became a learned class of wise men throughout Europe, respected and feared by the Romans.

About a thousand years after the Celts came another wave from the eastern steppes, the Teutonic or Germanic peoples, who conquered all Europe and finally conquered Rome. They were the Angles, Saxons and Jutes who went into England, the Franks who went into France, the Goths who invaded Spain and Italy. They were the last newcomers from the east into the continent of Europe, and out of the blend of all these peoples have come the arts, the languages and the peoples of Europe today.

Index